MW01005424

"As Jesus often used stories to great job of using vivid, real-l reality of spiritual warfare in important strategies for winning the battles we all face."

—Dr. Timothy Warner
Speaker, coauthor of *The Beginner's Guide to Spiritual Warfare*

⸺

"This book speaks, in real terms, about experiences in Vietnam. As a veteran of that war, I can assure you many like me look at that conflict—and the impact it has had on their lives—in ways the average American does not...Most importantly, the book sensitizes readers to the need to have a spiritual warfare battle plan for their own success."

—Dick Abel
Brig Gen, USAF (Ret.),
Executive Director, Military Ministry, Campus Crusade for Christ

⸺

"*Battle Plan for Spiritual Warfare* will equip you to be prepared for whatever the enemy brings against you. And most important, it will instill in you a deeper love and loyalty for the King of Kings."

—Steve McVey
author of *Grace Walk, Grace Amazing,* and *A Divine Invitation*

⸺

"*Battle Plan* offers insight into God's undying love, whose patience is evident even in the darkest of hours of wartime. It reminds us we are not alone in this world combating the many forces that threaten our daily walk with the Lord. A powerful message of faith, determination and, ultimately, love."

—Mikey L. Hoeven
First Lady of North Dakota

"Not only does *Battle Plan for Spiritual Warfare* have balance and biblical foundations that will help any Christian deal with the spiritual battles of life, but it has a message of healing insight that every soldier and war veteran will find compelling. Its message of hope is a much needed word for our time."

—**Mark Bubeck**
Biblical counselor, author of *Overcoming the Adversary*

"Joe and Rich have given us a much needed book for the body of Christ, which is often caught off guard by Satan's schemes to derail our spiritual lives. Every believer should make this book part of their equipping process."

—**Os Hillman**
President, Marketplace Leaders and International Coalition of Workplace Ministries

"I found myself consistently moved to a greater sense of urgency in my own spiritual battles...A story of spiritual hope."

—**Dr. Rick Dunn**
author; senior pastor of Fellowship Evangelical Free Church, Knoxville, TN

"A must-read guidebook for all who long for a victorious Christian life."
—**Dr. Benjamin Sawatsky**
Executive Director, Evangelical Free Church of America International Mission

BATTLE PLAN FOR
SPIRITUAL WARFARE

Joe Wasmond and **Rich Miller**

HARVEST HOUSE PUBLISHERS

EUGENE, OREGON

Cover by Left Coast Design, Portland, Oregon

Cover images ©: Siqui Sanchez/The Image Bank/Getty Images; C Squared Studios/Photodisc Green/Getty Images

The song "Hero of My Soul" on pages 5 and 6 is © Copyright 2003 Meadowgreen Music Company (ASCAP). All rights administered by EMI Christian Music Publishing.

The words of General Harold Moore on page 171 are taken from *We Were Soldiers Once...and Young* (New York: Random House, 1992), page xxi.

BATTLE PLAN FOR SPIRITUAL WARFARE
Copyright © 2004 by Joe Wasmond and Rich Miller
Published by Harvest House Publishers
Eugene, Oregon 97402
www.harvesthousepublishers.com

Library of Congress Cataloging-in-Publication Data

Wasmond, Joe, 1949-
   Battle plan for spiritual warfare / Joe Wasmond and Rich Miller.
      p. cm.
   Includes bibliographical references.
   ISBN 0-7369-1453-6 (pbk.)
   1. Spiritual warfare.   I. Miller, Rich, 1954—   II. Title.
   BV4509.5.W374 2004
   235'.4—dc22   2004004445

Printed in the United States of America

05   06   07   08   09   10   11   /   BP-MS   /   10   9   8   7   6   5   4   3

Rich's and my sentiments about this book are expressed
by the words from a new song by Michael and Marcee Merritt.
It is entitled *Hero of My Soul.*
To Him be all the praise, honor, and glory!

*Hero of my soul
You left your mark on me
The way you lived your life
Makes me want to be*

*Like my father
Bold against injustice
Tender to children
Free to be everything you are—*

Refrain:
*I'll never forget you
Hero of my soul
I gladly surrender
To the Hero of my soul*

Unapproachable light
Invited me to come
The king of all that's right
Called me his own son

Undeserved mercy
The way that you loved her
When everyone else had a rock in their hand
And wanted to kill her

You are the bravest soldier
You are the greatest servant
You are the perfect savior
O Hero of my soul

Refrain:
I'll never forget you
Hero of my soul
I gladly surrender
To the Hero of my soul

Michael and Marcee Merritt
are nationally known recording artists and songwriters.
They are partnering with Freedom in Christ Ministries
on a new CD of worship songs.

Contents

Foreword

The USS *Breckenridge* slowly made its way into Pearl Harbor. I was sailing on this troop transport to catch my ship, the USS *Leonard F. Mason,* which was stationed in Japan. My shipmates and I were standing at parade rest as we slipped past the remnants of the USS *Arizona*—a mute testimony to those who gave their lives in the service of their country. As we entered our berth, the Marine band on the pier was playing "Anchors Aweigh" and other patriotic songs. Dignitaries on board apparently warranted this special greeting.

I was a lonely country boy a long way from home, and I was feeling a little embarrassed by the tears that were rolling down my cheeks until I stole a glance at the other sailors and doggies who were lining the rail. They too were fighting back the tears. What is it about our human nature that longs for freedom and responds so deeply to those who give their lives to preserve it?

Three years later our sister ships, the *Turner Joy* and the *Maddox,* retaliated against North Vietnamese gunboats, an event that ignited the Vietnam conflict. I will never forget the fall of 1964, when our ship was assigned to the Gulf of Tonkin, and I woke up one morning to see the entire horizon dotted with troop transports ready to land thousands of soldiers. My tour of duty lasted just long enough for me to receive a Vietnam campaign ribbon. In the following years many good soldiers gave their lives because they were obedient in doing their duty and serving their country. Sadly though, many of our soldiers were treated dishonorably upon returning home.

Years later, in the Philippines I toured Corregidor, a tiny island that guarded the entrance into Manila Bay. I saw the Bataan Peninsula, where thousands of American and Filipino soldiers marched to their death. In the suburbs of Manila is a World War II memorial commemorating the 40,000-plus soldiers and sailors who gallantly gave their lives. We were all left speechless as we read their names, which were etched in stone slabs forming a large circle, and saw the crosses on the beautifully landscaped lawn. The spiritual significance of that memorial couldn't be missed by even the most callous observer. The centerpiece of the display was a monument to the glory of God.

I saw the same spiritual connection when I toured the War Memorial in Edinburgh, Scotland. Holding the central spot was a replica of the Ark of the Covenant with Michael the Archangel standing guard. The citizens of democratic countries in this world enjoy their political freedom because fathers and mothers have sacrificed their sons and daughters. Most would have gone in their place if they could have. Citizens of heaven likewise enjoy their spiritual freedom because our heavenly Father has sacrificed His only begotten Son so that we may live a liberated life in Christ. Freedom always costs somebody something—and when the cause is just, the price is always worth it.

The apostle Paul said it was for freedom that Christ set us free (Galatians 5:1). Every born-again believer is alive and free in Christ and is a citizen of heaven, but not many are living out what they are. What a tragedy, since that is the birthright of every child of God. Helping Christians be established alive and free in Christ through genuine repentance and faith in God has been the driving force of Freedom in Christ Ministries since its inception. Side by side with many others, we take part in the battle for the souls of humanity—an invisible spiritual war being fought between the kingdom of darkness and the kingdom of God's dear Son. There is much at stake since, according to the apostle John, the whole world lies in the power of the evil one (1 John 5:19). There are casualties everywhere.

Drawing from his tour of duty in Vietnam as a highly decorated helicopter pilot, Joe Wasmond, along with Rich Miller, shows the parallels between military strategies and the marching orders given to the army of God. These two men are "freedom fighters"—instruments in the hands of God who are being used to bind up the broken hearts of wounded warriors—and they are setting captives free all over the world.

Too many Christians are like blindfolded warriors who don't know who their enemy is, so they strike out at themselves and one another. This powerful book will help remove the blindfold and give you a better view of this fallen world from God's perspective. When you chose by faith to have your name written in the Lamb's Book of Life, you enlisted in God's eternal army, and the war you are in is winnable. So come on, soldier— put on the full armor of God, learn how to stand firm, and become a freedom fighter for the cause of Christ!

> —Neil T. Anderson
> Founder and President Emeritus of
> Freedom in Christ Ministries

About the Authors

During his service in Vietnam as a helicopter pilot from 1969 to 1970, **Joe Wasmond** was decorated with two Distinguished Flying Crosses, the Bronze Star Medal, and 42 Air Medals.

He and his wife, Kathy, were married in 1970 and came to Christ in 1977. Beginning in 1983 they spent extensive time in Africa, Guatemala, and Miami, Florida, as missionaries with the Evangelical Free Church Mission.

Joe and Kathy began serving with Freedom in Christ Ministries in 1995 as International Directors, and in 2001 Joe succeeded Neil Anderson as President of the organization. The Wasmonds' work spreading the message of freedom and reconciliation has taken them to more than 40 countries. Joe holds a Doctor of Ministry in Missiology degree from Trinity International University. He and Kathy now make their home in eastern Tennessee.

Rich Miller is an author and speaker for Freedom in Christ Ministries and a man whose heart beats for renewal and revival in the church. After meeting Christ as a college student, Rich spent 17 years with Campus Crusade for Christ, including a year as a traveling intern with Josh McDowell and two-plus years as a missionary to the Philippines. He and his wife, Shirley, were married in 1989.

In 1993 he joined Freedom in Christ Ministries at the invitation of Dr. Neil Anderson and since that time has been serving God by spreading the message of freedom around the world, including such places as Mongolia, China, Siberia, Ukraine, Thailand, and Liberia.

As a writer, he has authored or coauthored 13 books with Neil Anderson and others, including the popular *Freedom from Fear, Getting Anger Under Control,* and *Breaking the Bondage of Legalism* and the youth books *Reality Check* and *Awesome God* (an ECPA Gold Medallion finalist). Rich lives with his wife and four children in the mountains of western North Carolina.

The Fight of Our Lives

It was two days after Christmas 1969. The night was very black as we patrolled the skies over the jungles and rice paddies northwest of Saigon, South Vietnam (now called Ho Chi Minh City). All was quiet as I (Joe) turned our Nighthawk helicopter gunship around and headed back to the Cu Chi base camp to refuel.

Cu Chi was a small farming community in South Vietnam, about 18 miles from the Cambodian border. The enormous U.S. Army base camp built there during the Vietnam conflict was headquarters for the Second Brigade of the Twenty-fifth Infantry's Tropic Lightning Division—and also our home.

One of the largest army bases in Vietnam, Cu Chi stood strategically between the North Vietnamese–Vietcong strongholds to the north and Saigon to the south, thus making it also one of the most dangerous installations during the war. Saigon was, at the time, the capital of South Vietnam, and the enemy's prime objective. As U.S. soldiers we were called to work with the local population to help them fight for and build their own democratic society and government, seeking to engage the enemy in the heart of Vietcong-controlled territory.

I was assigned to Company A of the Twenty-fifth Aviation Battalion. Along with Companies B and C, we flew any mission necessary for the support of our ground troops and filled a vital role in providing them with air mobility. Together, all three companies logged nearly 4000 flying hours per month. Our motto was "We fly for the troops."

Our call sign was the "Little Bears," named after a honey bear captured and given to us by a special forces unit that our aviation company had extracted from a hot landing zone some years earlier. The image of the bear standing upright, clutching a lightning bolt, was embossed on the Twenty-Fifth Infantry Division shoulder patches and stenciled on the noses and side panels of our helicopters. My personal call sign was "Little Bear 21," which I received in 1969 at age 19, after becoming an aircraft commander just a few months into my tour of duty.

Our mission that night was to provide gunship cover to protect the troops on the ground, including the numerous six-man ambush patrols scattered across the landscape below us. From our vantage point they appeared dug in and secure for the night.

Suddenly we saw tracer rounds from our own M-16s and enemy AK-47 rifles spewing in all directions. An ambush patrol, one of the units from the Second Battalion of the Fourteenth Infantry, was under serious attack. As we tuned in the battalion's radio frequency, the patrol leader was already calling for help. We could hear the sounds of close combat in our headsets as he keyed in his microphone. A much larger force had engaged them and their position was now being overrun by Vietcong (VC) soldiers. We abandoned our vector, banked hard 180 degrees, and entered the battle zone below.

As soon as we arrived, we ejected flares enabling us and the ground units to see the attacking forces. We dove down from 3000 feet in a high overhead circling descent, firing our minigun around the perimeter of our troop position. This weapon could deliver 4000 to 6000 rounds per minute, and our gunner had to be careful not to hit our own people. All he had to guide him was the strobe light flashing from the helmet of one of our soldiers sitting in a foxhole on the ground below. I was focused on maneuvering our helicopter in this accelerated descent to get down to the landing zone (LZ) and get our troops out of there.

As we neared the LZ under the illumination of the flares, we observed enemy soldiers running freely through our intended touchdown point. Turning on our landing lights at the last minute, we received such intense VC fire that we had to pull out.

By this time two of our soldiers were already dead and several more severely wounded. Other gunship helicopters were coming on site, but we needed help to extract our men. We radioed for more air and artillery support. F-4 Phantom jets that had been scrambled out of Tan Son Nhut airbase in Saigon arrived overhead, ready to drop napalm on both sides of the LZ, while our heavy artillery fire pounded the perimeter around our troops.

We coordinated our approach with the Phantoms and raced in just behind their bombing runs. I quickly dropped our helicopter toward the ground. As we landed, the heat from the napalm fire whooshed through our open cargo bays. The men who were left from this six-man patrol came running toward my aircraft, carrying the dead and wounded bodies of their comrades. They were followed by VC soldiers firing at us. Their bullets and mortar were exploding within yards of our helicopter. We shut off our landing lights and depended on the flares overhead to get our bearings.

I pulled out my own weapon and began firing from the side door of the cockpit. I had no expectations of leaving that LZ alive, but we were not going to take off without trying our best to get our men out of this hostile situation…even if it meant dying with them right there.

As our soldiers struggled to board the chopper, I noticed one of them was missing a portion of his leg, with a tourniquet tied around his thigh to stop the bleeding. He was hoisted into our cargo bay. Heroically, one of his squad members rushed back into the LZ, retrieved his missing leg with the boot still attached, and jumped into the helicopter, firing his M-16 with his free hand. The risk he took was not foolish. Our doctors and nurses back at the base-camp field hospital had become miracle workers in repairing severed body parts, and so chances were good this man's leg could be saved. It was well worth the wait in this hot LZ.

Dumping the remainder of our flares and ammunition in order to lighten our weight for takeoff, we got out of there as fast as we could. Our skids bounced off the ground several times and we dragged through the grass before getting airborne. Seconds later we gained altitude and were soon wrapped in the safety of the dark skies, out of the reach of the enemy below.

One month later I was awarded the Distinguished Flying Cross (DFC) for this action. I wasn't thinking of medals that dangerous night, or on any other mission I flew for that matter. My only concern was for my fellow soldiers I was called and equipped to support. We were all just operating as a team, doing what our commander in chief had ordered us to do.

The commendation they awarded me read as follows:

> Receiving word that several friendly casualties had been sustained, Warrant Officer Wasmond fearlessly landed in a hostile area. With complete disregard for his own safety, Warrant Officer Wasmond exposed himself to the hail of fire as he remained in the perilous area until all the wounded were aboard his aircraft. His valorous actions contributed immeasurably to the success of the mission. Warrant Officer Wasmond's bravery and devotion to duty are in keeping with the highest tradition of military service and reflect great credit upon himself, his unit, the 25th Infantry Division, and the United States Army. By direction of the President, under the provision of the Congress of the United States.

Six months later, on June 6, 1970, I was awarded a second DFC, for rescuing a downed and wounded pilot involved in resupply operations. Though the ground element had notified me that there was not adequate room for a safe landing, I carefully hovered down through the trees and landed anyway. It never occurred to me not to rescue the man, even though the enemy fire was dangerous. Again, I was just doing what my fellow soldiers would have done for me.

I never found out who put in the DFC citations. As I read the commendations today, more than 30 years later, in the safety and quiet of my home, I find it hard to remember that I acted as cited. All I know is that it never occurred to me *not* to come to the aid of a fellow soldier.

In retrospect, I now know that God was preparing me, even before I knew Him, to bring Him glory by rescuing wounded and captive souls. It has become my mission in life to help people be established free and complete in Christ so they can joyfully obey the Great Commandment (to love God and people) in order to fulfill their role in accomplishing the Great Commission (to make disciples of all nations).

Writing this book has not been easy. I have had to face a lot of painful memories that I would much rather have ignored or forgotten. But it also has been a healing time for me. If you were one of those stationed in Southeast Asia between 1959 and 1975, or if you have been deployed in any other war, I am asking God that He would make this book part of your healing journey as well.

If you have been graciously spared from military combat, my request to the Lord is that He would enable you to translate my wartime experiences into your present-day reality so you can understand that we are all engaged in the fight of our lives. It is a spiritual battle where we, as children of God, are called to take His truth in love to a world of increasing, encroaching darkness. As much as we might not want to face it, the truth is that every one of us lives each day of our lives on a cosmic battlefield called planet Earth.

John Eldredge, in his book *Waking the Dead*, reminds us of the powerful theme of warfare against evil, which fills our culture and literature:

Little Red Riding Hood is attacked by a wolf. Dorothy must face and bring down the Wicked Witch of the West. Qui-Gon Jinn and Obi-Wan Kenobi go hand to hand against Darth Maul. To release the captives of the Matrix, Neo battles the powerful "agents." Frodo is hunted by the Black Riders... Beowulf kills the monster Grendel, and then he has to battle Grendel's mother. Saint George slays the dragon. The children who stumbled into Narnia are called upon by Aslan to battle the White Witch and her armies so that Narnia might be free. Every story has a villain because *yours* does. You were born into a world at war.[1]

Our Strategy and Objective

When Rich and I began praying about and planning this book, at first we felt strongly we should write a sort of primer on spiritual warfare, one specifically designed for men. It still is our deep desire that this book will open up men's eyes, ears, and hearts to the reality of spiritual conflict with a foe who is trying to steal, kill, and destroy lives, marriages, families, churches, and even nations. Both of us are asking God to make men better equipped and more motivated to take their place of leadership and engage the enemy effectively in battle as a result of what we have written.

But we have also waged spiritual battle shoulder to shoulder with brave, godly women—especially our wives—and so Rich and I have written this book for our sisters in Christ as well. My two daughters, Jennifer and Sarah, have both made significant contributions to and given valuable input for this book, and we have concluded it with an epilogue from my dear wife, Kathy, who has given her perspective on a journey that has intimately involved her. She has been my friend and wife, the mother of our two daughters, and my partner in serving God and His people for well over 30 years.

Each chapter begins with an incident from my life, including some of my combat experiences in Vietnam. These stories serve as illustrations for the teaching and encouragement from the Bible that follows—which, we hope, will provide some basic tracks to run on as you grapple with the reality of the invisible war against the world, the flesh, and the devil in your life.

Then, at the end of each chapter we have added a few tools. First, a prayer you can pray to ask the Lord to make the truths of that chapter real in your life. Following that, a Scripture reading that will enable you to go deeper into those truths. And lastly, to make this book useful for couples, home fellowship groups, men's studies, Sunday school classes, and so on, a series of questions for discussion. If you are reading this book on your own, those same questions can prompt some very valuable personal reflection as well.

What we want, and what we are asking God, is that this book would provide you with a motivational and practical battle plan for spiritual warfare.

War is coming. It is, in fact, already here. The war started ages ago in a beautiful garden called Eden (Genesis 3), and it will not be over until Jesus comes a second time to make all things new.

The question is not whether you are in a war. The question is, "Are you prepared for battle?"

1
This Means War!

Nine years old is an awfully young age to go to war, but it was then that I first experienced the reality of the spiritual battle. It was 1959, and I was being raised in a Catholic home, school, and church environment that taught me many important truths about God...but also taught me that if I wasn't good the devil would come during the night to "get me." Somehow that fear tactic failed to accomplish its purpose, as I was usually in more than my share of trouble!

As I recall, that particular year our family was living in a house without enough bedrooms for all of us. My four sisters, who were younger, slept in the upstairs bedrooms, while I slept in an attic area above the kitchen. It was a dark, unfinished space that would have frightened any young child.

My parents had just put us to bed and turned out the lights. I was trying to sleep, buried completely under my covers, when I felt an evil presence in the room. I dared to peek out from under the bedspread, and there in the corner of the attic was a dark shadow. I froze with terror as I sensed it wanted to harm me.

After what seemed like hours, I mustered up enough courage to run from the attic to the first-floor bedroom where my parents were sleeping. I wanted so much to open their door and jump into bed with them, but I was afraid they would find my fear unfounded and foolish. After all, I was their oldest—and as a boy nine years of age I needed to be beyond these childish night-terror experiences.

So I hid myself under the dining room table—which was just outside their door—until dawn. This went on for months, until we finally moved from that house into a larger one with sufficient space to house six more brothers and sisters yet to be born.

Fast-forward to 1974. I had been married to Kathy for four years, after serving three in the U.S. Army including a one-year tour of duty in Vietnam. I owned my own construction business. Our first daughter was two years old, and life seemed to be on the upswing.

A new movie, *The Exorcist*, had just come out in theaters and foolishly I went to see it. For the first time, in cinematographic detail, I saw my childhood terrors portrayed on a movie screen. I was traumatized by what I saw but could not share my fears with my wife. For years I had been having nightmares from my experiences in Vietnam that caused me to wake up many nights screaming, but this night I would awaken for another reason.

I was restless much of the night, and around three o'clock in the morning I became aware of an evil presence in our bedroom. It looked and felt the same as the presence I had experienced when I was nine years old. I was so startled by what I saw that I cried out with fear, waking up Kathy. I lied, telling her that it was just another nightmare—but I was shaken to the core knowing that the evil presence from my childhood had returned to haunt me.

Six years later, in 1980, we moved to the north woods of Wisconsin. Three years before, Kathy and I had both received the Lord in a Baptist church in Elgin, Illinois, and now we were eager new believers looking for a church—though it took visiting more than ten churches over a two-year period to finally find our spiritual home.

During our second visit to the Evangelical Free church in Conover, Wisconsin—the church we would eventually join—I sensed that same evil presence I had met before. I was outraged and confused. I had believed that as a Christian I would never again have to encounter such horrible fear.

When I approached the pastor—a 20-year missionary veteran with the Free Church Mission in Zaire (now Congo), Africa—he explained that he and the church elders had been helping one of their members, who had been involved in satanism. They were trying to free this professing believer from the demonic influences in her life. The pastor also suggested I might have the gift of discerning spirits. At that time in my life I had no clue what he was talking about, and I was quite sure I wanted nothing to do with it either!

Also during this same time period, our eldest daughter began waking up almost every night with what we can only describe as bizarre night-terror experiences. She was convinced there was something very frightening in her room, and she could not sleep. We spent many sleepless nights trying to comfort her without much success. As I was forced to watch my precious girl go through the same terrors I had gone through as a child, it would have been an understatement to say that I was discouraged.*

Neither Ignorance nor Fascination

The experiences I described bring us to a main focus of our first chapter: launching a preemptive strike against one of the more common maladies associated with the study of spiritual warfare. This is, namely, either pretending that there is no spiritual battle going on and sticking our heads in the sand (like I was doing) or attributing all our problems to the demonic. C.S. Lewis, in the preface to his classic work *The Screwtape Letters* puts it this way:

> There are two equal and opposite errors into which our race can fall about the devils. One is to disbelieve in their existence. The other is to believe, and to feel an excessive and unhealthy interest in them. They themselves are equally pleased by both errors and hail a materialist or a magician with the same delight.[2]

---

* To understand how a biblical worldview can help explain night terrors and night-time apparitions, see the appendix.

Chances are slim that you are a disbeliever in the spiritual world or you would likely have tossed this book aside by now. The second temptation that Lewis warns against is much more subtle, however, and therefore presents a real and present danger.

When a Christian begins to understand the reality of the spirit realm and our authority in Christ, it is so liberating that he or she can overdose on it all. An overzealous believer can end up rebuking demons where there are none and foolishly charging into battles he or she is neither called nor equipped to fight. The pendulum swings to extremes more easily than you might imagine. It is true that Scripture warns us to "be of sober spirit, be on the alert. Your adversary, the devil, prowls around like a roaring lion, seeking someone to devour" (1 Peter 5:8). But note first Peter's use of the word "sober." We are to be alert, not excitable and unstable. More crucially, though, we are to fix our eyes on Jesus, the author and perfecter of our faith (Hebrews 12:2), not on Satan, and we are to "keep seeking the things above, where Christ is, seated at the right hand of God" (Colossians 3:1), not on the things of earth where demons are.

If you are a child of God, you have already been seated in the heavenly realm, far above evil principalities and dark powers (Ephesians 2:6). The only way that Satan and his forces can take advantage of you is if you believe his lies and accusations or give in to his temptations to sin.

The Starting Point

When Jesus finished His all-night prayer vigil on the mountain and then summoned those He had chosen as apostles, His reasons for choosing them provide a healthy framework for all of us in keeping our spiritual priorities in order:

> And He appointed twelve, so that they would be with Him and that He could send them out to preach, and to have authority to cast out the demons (Mark 3:14-15).

Jesus' first priority for the Twelve and for us is *to be with Him*—to be in intimate, growing relationship with Him. This must always be at the top of the list for any believer in Christ to be spiritually healthy and balanced. You can't love Jesus too much! But it is dangerously easy to allow other things—especially serving God's family and even spiritual warfare—to become our first love.

The apostle John relayed a message from the Lord Jesus Himself to the church at Ephesus (see Revelation 2:1-7). This city was a hotbed for spiritual warfare in the first century mainly because of the citizens' rabid devotion to the pagan goddess Artemis, whose temple, one of the seven wonders of the ancient world, was located just outside the city.

Jesus' letter to the Ephesian believers commended them for their hard work and endurance in trial and even their intolerance of evil men and false apostles (see verses 1-3). Quite a résumé! But what they had missed in all their *labor* for Jesus was a *love* for Jesus, and He threatened to shut the whole operation down if they didn't get that one thing right (verses 4-5).

That's why Jesus' first purpose for calling the Twelve was primarily for them to be with Him in relationship, and then secondarily *that He could send them out to preach.* After we get our *love* in the right place, then our *labor* in serving other people is important—vitally important. Ephesians 2:10 even says that we are God's "workmanship, created in Christ Jesus for good works, which God prepared beforehand so that we would walk in them." God made us for good works! But our responsibility is to walk with Jesus who will lead us into the good works that He has already prepared for us to do. If we're not walking with Jesus, we'll end up doing our own thing and not His. God's good works for us always flow from an abiding relationship with Christ (see John 15:1-8).

Finally, as we are walking with Jesus and preaching the good news, we will encounter the powers of darkness and those held captive by them. Count on it. And so the Lord Jesus bestowed on the apostles and on us *authority to cast out the demons.* We'll talk later about a methodology of how to do that effectively, but for now it's enough to say that dealing with the demonic, though important, is never to be our primary or even secondary focus.

Complacency: A Bad Strategy

All the above said, why have we written this book?

Good question. First, it is for the reason we mentioned earlier. We are all engaged in the fight of our lives on this cosmic battlefield called planet Earth. But many Christians are choosing to keep their heads in the sand, which brings us to our second reason: The apostle Paul's assertion that "we are not ignorant of his [Satan's] schemes" cannot honestly be made by a large portion of the Church in the Western world. Too many of us *are* ignorant of the devil's schemes, and therefore he is able to take advantage of us (see 2 Corinthians 2:11). What starts out as an enemy *foothold* today can one day become a *stronghold,* and eventually even a *stranglehold,* of control in the life of a believer in Christ. We are all vulnerable to deception…every one of us!

In the 1930s, Adolf Hitler was able to annex huge chunks of Europe step-by-step simply because leaders more powerful than him believed his lies, were not fully aware of his schemes, considered themselves beyond his reach, and—ultimately—were fearful of getting involved, hoping he would somehow just go away or leave them alone.

But complacency never defeats evil. It takes war.

Clinton Arnold, in his excellent book *Three Crucial Questions about Spiritual Warfare,* comments on the inevitability of war in the spiritual realm:

> Some believers are too frightened even to talk about spiritual warfare and thus try earnestly to avoid the topic altogether. Avoiding the topic is a profoundly inadequate response. Spiritual warfare is not an isolatable compartment of church ministry or Christian experience. Spiritual warfare is an

integral part of the entire Christian experience. It is a fact of life. To think that a Christian could avoid spiritual warfare is like imagining that a gardener could avoid dealing with weeds. Our goal should be to gain an accurate and sober-minded understanding of spiritual warfare—not a view tainted by frightening superstitions and odd practices.[3]

Arnold is right. Ignoring something doesn't make it go away, and avoiding spiritual warfare will become increasingly difficult in these last days before the return of the King. Jesus foretold that things will get even more intense as "false Christs and false prophets will arise and will show great signs and wonders, so as to mislead, if possible, even the elect. Behold, I have told you in advance" (Matthew 24:24-25).

The Battle for Our Minds

Why is it so crucial that we not ignore the war we are in? It's because a key linchpin of Satan's strategy is a full-front, vicious assault on mankind's understanding of who God is and who we are in relationship to Him.

Let us explain. Satan, working through his forces (demons), wants to make good things appear bad and bad things appear good, so that we'll reject the good and receive the bad. When tempting Eve in the Garden of Eden, he attacked God's goodness, slandering the truthfulness of His character. In response to God's warning that eating from the tree of the knowledge of good and evil would result in death (Genesis 2:17), the devil declared,

> *You surely will not die! For God knows that in the day you eat from it your eyes will be opened, and you will be like God, knowing good and evil* (3:4-5).

The devil's insinuations were clear: *You can't trust God. God is just looking out for Himself. He doesn't want you to experience all the good things in life, because He wants to keep you under His thumb.* In this case, human hindsight is 20/20. The devil was clearly lying, but Eve didn't see it.

Much of spiritual battle is won or lost on this very battlefield... the battlefield of our beliefs about God. What we believe or don't believe about God is the most important thing about us, and it really is a battle for our minds. Do we truly trust that God loves us, is good, and wants the best for us, even when life on this fallen planet hands us a raw deal? The devil and his forces will fight round-the-clock to convince us that faith in God is a waste of time.

Make no mistake. The powers of darkness hate God with a passion and so have unleashed a ferocious "no holds barred" attack on His most treasured creation, mankind. Demonic forces are hard at work trying to whisper lies into our minds to distort our picture of God. They will use any resource at their disposal, including false religions, deceived people, ungodly media (books, movies, computer and video games, music, news sources, and so on)—even direct communication into our minds—to try to implant their lies into our thinking. Have you ever battled with one or more of these images of God?

- God is so distant and uninterested, and busy with running planet Earth, He really doesn't have time for me. It's not really possible to have a close relationship with Him. He loves everybody, I guess—after all, that's His job—but deep down He doesn't really love *me*.

- God is severe and stern. Maybe even cruel and abusive. He doesn't want me to have fun here on Earth, and He frowns on me—and anybody—when we're enjoying life "too much."

- The only way to please God is to rigorously keep His commands. He is quick to notice when I fail and even quicker to bring punishment. He loves me when I'm good, but is very angry with me when I'm not.

- God doesn't expect me to be perfect. He knows I have vices just like everybody and is kind of like a kindly old grandfather. He just winks and looks the other way when I sin.

- There are many ways to God. All religions are basically the same. It doesn't matter which one I choose, just as long as I'm sincere.

The Way Out of Deception

Each one of these pictures of God is a distortion. If you have believed any of them, you have been deceived by the father of lies. The Bible reveals God's character to be "gracious and merciful, slow to anger and great in lovingkindness" (Psalm 145:8). He is not distant and unreachable, for the Scripture invites us to "seek the LORD while He may be found; call upon Him while He is near. Let the wicked forsake His way and the unrighteous man his thoughts; and let him return to the LORD, and He will have compassion on him, and to our God, for He will abundantly pardon" (Isaiah 55:6-7).

The way back to God is not confusing. It is simply through Jesus. He Himself said, "I am the way, and the truth, and the life; no one comes to the Father but through Me" (John 14:6).

The gospel *(gospel* means *good news)* is simple. God loves us. All of us have sinned, and that sin separates us from Him and His love. Jesus, God's beloved, one and only Son, died, and thus paid the penalty required by God for our sin. Jesus then rose from the dead, and now He offers us not only forgiveness of sin but an entirely new life. When we confess our sin and need for Jesus and open our hearts by faith to receive Him, He becomes the Leader (Lord), Forgiver (Savior) and Supply Line (Source) of our lives.

Our forgiveness and family relationship with God does not come through working hard to keep His commands. That is impossible, for all of us have already failed to measure up to His standard of perfection. But when we, by faith, receive God's free gift of forgiveness and life in Christ, the perfection of Jesus is credited to us—and we are put into God's family!

If you have never begun the most important relationship of your life—a rich, warm Father–child relationship with our loving God, provided through His Son, Jesus Christ—we want to give you that opportunity right now. If the Lord has opened your eyes and heart so you see your need for forgiveness and new life through Christ, we heartily welcome you to pray along with us:

> *Dear heavenly Father, I come to You with nothing to offer except my own sin and emptiness and my need for You to be merciful to me. I know that all my efforts to earn a place in Your family fall flat before Your holy perfection. In my helplessness to save myself, I look to Jesus only to forgive me and make me clean. Thank You for His death on the cross, which was the full payment for my sins. Thank You that because He rose from the dead, He can give me new life—His life. I renounce any and all allegiance to the ways and works of darkness, and I pledge my allegiance to the Lord Jesus alone. I receive Him—and by Your promise, Father, I now gratefully take my place in Your family as Your child, holy and dearly loved. Thank You for being merciful to me and saving me this day. In Jesus' powerful name I pray, amen.*

If you made this decision to receive Christ, welcome to the family of God! You have made the most important decision of your life, and we encourage you to share what you've done with another Christian you know and trust. He or she can help you begin growing in your faith. In addition, you are going to find the rest of this book very helpful to your newfound faith, especially the next chapter!

The Extent of Jesus' Victory

As vitally important as Jesus' saving us from sin is, it is not the whole story. He also came to deliver (rescue) us from the devil's rule in our lives. Christ accomplished that through His death, burial, and resurrection. Consider the following scriptures:

> *Since the children share in flesh and blood, He Himself likewise also partook of the same, that through death He might render powerless him who had the power of death, that is, the devil, and might free those who through fear of death were subject to slavery all their lives* (Hebrews 2:14-15).

> *The Son of God appeared for this purpose, to destroy the works of the devil* (1 John 3:8).

> *When you were [spiritually] dead in your transgressions and the uncircumcision of your flesh, He made you alive together with Him, having forgiven us all our transgressions, having canceled out the certificate of debt consisting of decrees against us, which was hostile to us; and He has taken it out of the way, having nailed it to the cross. When He disarmed the rulers and authorities [evil spiritual powers], He made a public display of them, having triumphed over them through Him* (Colossians 2:13-15).

Now that Jesus has utterly defeated sin, death, and the devil, we can (through Him) learn to win the daily battles against the schemes of the enemy. And that's what the rest of this book is all about.

You might still be wondering about that evil presence that haunted me (Joe) earlier in my life. It no longer concerns me because now I know who I am in Christ and how to repel such an attack. Had I known Christ then as I know Him today, I could have simply followed James 4:7, which says, "Submit therefore to God. Resist the devil and he will flee from you." In my heart I would have surrendered to God's lordship in my life and then verbally I would have told that thing, "Go, in Jesus' name!" And it would've been all over.

Sound too simple? Well, there's a lot more that goes along with being able to stand against the enemy so authoritatively. Remember, we've just begun our boot camp training for spiritual battle. The battle plan is not fully in place yet. In this chapter we've looked briefly at who God is and how we can be rightly related to Him. And we've caught a quick glimpse of our victorious Jesus. In the next chapter we'll learn more about our new identity—who we are in Christ—about our place in Him, and about how that opens the door for joining Him in His victory. Prepare to be encouraged!

Dear heavenly Father, what a good and true and holy and loving and faithful and merciful and powerful God You are! Despite all the lies about You that the devil has tried to get me to believe, I drive a stake in the ground right now and declare that I will trust in You no matter what. I have known that Your ways are different than mine, and at times I have been angry with You because You did not do things my way. But now I know that Your ways are higher than mine and that it should not surprise me when I do not fully grasp Your purposes. Instead of rebelling, I choose to rest in You. Instead of whining, I choose to worship. Instead of trying to make my own way, I choose to trust. Make straight paths for my feet, Lord, as I journey ahead, walking with You and waging—and by Your grace, winning—spiritual battle. In Jesus' name—Faithful and True—I pray, amen.

(Isaiah 55:9)

For further Scripture study on God's trustworthy character:

Immerse yourself for a few minutes in the awesome truths of Isaiah 40. (If fear has been a controlling force in your life, bathe in Psalm 91 as well!)

Questions for reflection and discussion:

Have you ever experienced a frightening supernatural presence? What does 1 Peter 5:7-8 tell us about the source of that fear? What does 1 Peter 5:8-10 tell us to do in such instances?

Why do you think the devil and his forces work so hard to erode your trust in God? If you distrust God, in what will you end up trusting? (See Proverbs 3:5-8.)

What can we do to help children overcome the fear attacks of the enemy? Why is it an inadequate response to simply turn on the light and tell a child there is nothing there to be afraid of? (See the appendix for more discussion on this.)

When fear controls us, we are unable to walk by faith in God, thus leaving us very vulnerable to the enemy's control. What do the following scriptures teach us about fear and the remedy for it? (Isaiah 41:10; 2 Timothy 1:7; Proverbs 3:21-26; Romans 8:14-16.)

2
The Child of God Is a Warrior

It was a cold February morning in 1968. America was rapidly deploying troops into the Vietnam conflict and the military draft was on. Born in 1949, my choices after my 1967 high school graduation were to attend college, dodge the draft by moving to Canada or claiming a fraudulent exemption, wait to be drafted, or voluntarily enlist in the army. Though I would never have deserted or lied to my country, neither was I interested in further education at that time. So, wanting a few more choices than the two million who would be drafted, I made the choice to sign up.

I enlisted in the U.S. Army at the Elgin, Illinois, recruiting office, and then went on to their processing center for a day of physical exams and aptitude tests designed to see if I qualified. At the end of the day they declared me fit for service. All of us who passed the tests that day were sworn into the army that very afternoon. I guess they wanted to make sure we didn't change our minds!

A few weeks later I would be heading off to basic training, or—as it was officially titled—"Initial-Entry Training." Everyone else called it "boot camp."

I was assigned to eight weeks at the army base in Fort Leonard Wood, Missouri. Boot camp can be a scary experience. It was designed as mind training to tear down our individual civilian identity and replace it with a corporate, military one. We were allowed to bring only one suitcase with specifically designated items of clothing and toiletries. You didn't dare bring anything more to boot camp than what was allowed.

I said my farewells to my family the night before I left. The next morning my father dropped me off at the army pickup station. We hugged each other and said goodbye. From his experience in World War II he knew what I was headed for, though I didn't. I will always remember the look on his face as I stepped onto that bus. He was sending his firstborn son to fight for freedom…freedoms that we enjoyed as a nation and that were now in jeopardy in a country 12,000 miles away. He knew it might mean laying down my life and never seeing me alive again.

This was one of the loneliest times of my life. I think I saw tears running down my father's cheeks that day as he walked away from the bus. I will never fully understand what it cost him that day, but I was glad he was there with me.

I will spare you the tiresome details of boot camp. It *was* tiresome—not to mention repetitious and at times humiliating. There was nothing glamorous about it, though there would be a significant measure of satisfaction in having made it through. A large portion of our time was taken up with marching, drill ceremonies, lots of standing very still in formation, running, pushups, shooting, physical and emotional training (including being yelled at a lot!), discipline to detail, and learning how to use our weapons to defeat the enemy.

The goal was not so much to train us to be killers as it was to teach us to work as a team in order to accomplish a mission. The mission as we knew it was to help the helpless and to make sure each team member came back alive. Where the enemy stood in the way, he would have to be removed.

～

Both the marines and the army now have distinctive ways of bringing boot camp to a close—a 54-to-72-hour marathon of food and sleep deprivation, marching, and training exercises. The marines

call it "The Crucible." The army at Fort Jackson, South Carolina, calls
their event "Victory Forge," and all other army basic-training sites have
something similar.

In a Department of Defense article describing the transformation
that takes place through basic training, one marine stated,

> We are not just giving them basic training, we're turning them
> into Marines. There is more to being a Marine than knowing
> how to fire a weapon. There is an entire tradition behind it,
> and we want these recruits to measure up to the men and
> women who went before them.[4]

Commenting on the culmination of U.S. Army basic training,
General John A. Van Alstyne of Fort Jackson said,

> Soldiers now feel like they are pushed both physically and
> mentally, and they are proud of what they have done. Training
> companies routinely come out of Victory Forge looking like
> rifle platoons that just finished two days of combat operations.
> When the drill sergeants walk down the line and congratu-
> late the soldiers, telling them that they have done a good job,
> many of them break down and cry. They are being told this
> by someone they really respect. It means a lot to them.[5]

Fort Jackson's Victory Forge ends at night. The soldiers gather
around a fiery forge, and as the flames shoot out of the pit, the battalion commander puts their basic-training experiences into perspective. He holds up a steel rod and tells them that they came to boot
camp with much potential, but still unshaped. But now, to mark the
completion of their initiation into the army by finishing this last test
of basic training, he symbolically drops the steel rod, reaches into the
forge, and pulls out a fine-tooled sword.

Up until that moment, the men and women are called "recruits."
But as the commander pulls the sword out from the flames, for the
first time he calls them "soldiers." They have made it—they truly belong

and now they really know it! The relief, joy, and satisfaction are overwhelming as those words of affirmation are spoken.

Learning to Accept What the Father Says About You

How many of God's people are living life trying desperately to "make it," to gain some kind of assurance they truly belong to God's family and are accepted by Him and acceptable to Him? To be able to hear one clear word of affirmation from the Father's heart that they are loved and lovable would bring them immeasurable relief, unquenchable joy, and incredible satisfaction of soul.

Perhaps that is you today. You know that God is *supposed* to love you, because the Bible says He loves everybody, right? You can quote John 3:16 backward and forward…and yet whatever love you sense from the Father seems locked in your head, unable to resonate in your heart.

We wish we could toss a spiritual hand grenade and blast away any wall of guilt, shame, unworthiness, bitterness, or unbelief that blocks God's truth from entering into your heart, but we can't. That you must do yourself as you reject any lies you've believed, embrace God's truth, confess any sins you've committed, and forgive all who have hurt you. But we are praying—even while we write—that as you continue reading this book, God will bring a breakthrough that will enable you to shout your "Amen!" to the truth that "you have not received a spirit of slavery leading to fear again, but you have received a spirit of adoption as sons by which we cry out, 'Abba! Father!'" and that you will sense that "the Spirit Himself testifies with our spirit that we are children of God" (Romans 8:15-16).

This is supremely important. In order for us to wage war as victorious soldiers of Christ, we must first know that we are dearly loved children of God. Only that rock-solid assurance of our right standing with God and His deep delight in us will give us the security of soul to effectively engage the enemy in battle.

Prior to listing the armor of God available to each believer in Christ, Paul writes these words in Ephesians 6:10:

> *Be strong* in the Lord *and in the strength of His might.*

You cannot be strong *in the Lord* if you do not know what it means to be "in the Lord." That's the whole theme of Ephesians chapter 1. In Christ—in union with Him—we are saints, blessed with every spiritual blessing, chosen by Him to be holy, lovingly adopted by Him in kindness, lavishly given His grace, accepted, redeemed, forgiven, and given a wonderful inheritance (see Ephesians 1:1-12)! And He has sealed the whole deal by giving us the Holy Spirit of promise (verses 13-14).

The Best Kind of News

Are you beginning to get the message that you are not a *recruit*—but a treasured child of God, handpicked to serve in the greatest army there ever was, the army of King Jesus?

Why not take a moment and pray for yourself, as the apostle Paul wrote, that God

> *would grant you, according to the riches of His glory, to be strengthened with power through His Spirit in the inner man, so that Christ may dwell in your hearts through faith; and that you, being rooted and grounded in love, may be able to comprehend with all the saints what is the breadth and length and height and depth, and to know the love of Christ which surpasses knowledge, that you may be filled up to all the fullness of God* (Ephesians 3:16-19).

And in this, as the following verse declares, we have the assurance that He is "able to do far more abundantly beyond all that we ask or think, according to the power that works within us"!

We cannot say this any more passionately: *If you have trusted Christ alone to save you from your sins, then you're in! You belong! You are accepted and acceptable to God. You are a member in good standing of the Father's family and He loves you just like He loves His Son, Jesus!* Not convinced yet? Read on...

> *Just as the Father has loved Me, I have loved you; abide in My love* (Jesus' words in John 15:9).
>
> *...I in them and You in Me, that they may be perfected in unity, so that the world may know that You sent Me, and loved them, even as You have loved Me* (Jesus' prayer in John 17:23).
>
> *See how great a love the Father has bestowed on us, that we would be called children of God; and such we are...Beloved, now we are children of God* (John writing in 1 John 3:1,2).
>
> *As high as the heavens are above the earth, so great is His lovingkindness toward those who fear Him. As far as the east is from the west, so far has He removed our transgressions from us. Just as a father has compassion on his children, so the LORD has compassion on those who fear Him* (King David's words in Psalm 103:11-13).

Many times we feel utterly unworthy of such lavish, affectionate love from God because we know how often and how awfully we sin. But His love for us does not fluctuate like the Dow Jones industrial average. It is not based on how well or poorly we performed spiritually today, yesterday, or any day. It is based on His unchanging nature (see James 1:17)—and His nature is to love because He *is* love (1 John 4:15-17).

More of the Best Kind of News

At this point you, like many believers in Christ, may still be unsure. You've heard Jeremiah 17:9, which says "the heart is more deceitful than all else and is desperately sick"...and if your heart is like that, how could God possibly love you?

Let's set the record straight. Jeremiah's description of the human heart is accurate for someone without Christ, but it is not meant to be a diagnosis of the heart of you, a new-covenant follower of Jesus. Ezekiel 36:25-28 describes what happened when you turned to the Lord:

> *I [God] will sprinkle clean water on you, and you will be clean; I will cleanse you from all your filthiness and from all your idols. Moreover, I will give you a* new heart *and put a new spirit within you; and I will* remove the heart of stone from your flesh and give you a heart of flesh. *I will put My Spirit within you and cause you to walk in My statutes, and you will be careful to observe My ordinances.*

You, just like every believer in Christ at the moment of salvation, were transformed into an entirely new person. You were given a new, soft heart. You were given a new, alive spirit. And the Holy Spirit came to live inside you so that your body is now called "a temple of the Holy Spirit" (1 Corinthians 6:19). You could not ask for greater dignity to be granted to your body than for God Himself to make it His home!

Second Corinthians 5:17 puts it in a nutshell: "If anyone is in Christ, he is a new creature; the old things passed away; behold, new things have come." In reality, Christians are a whole new species of humanity that has never existed before, for we are people that have the living presence of the Living Christ, dwelling Spirit-to-spirit with us!

Under the old covenant (Old Testament), the Spirit of God would come *upon* people (kings, prophets, and so on) for the purpose of service. In Christ, under the new covenant, the Spirit of God has come to dwell *within* people for the purpose of transforming them from the inside out.

One of the devil's favorite lies to tell to Christians is this: He makes them think that deep down they are really the same person they always were…but they just happen to be going to heaven now.

That's why it really upsets us when we hear people saying, "Oh, I'm just a wicked old sinner saved by grace." In essence they're saying, "I'm nothing, nothing, nothing. I'm just the dirt under the little toenail of the body of Christ."

Give us a break! That's not you at all! You *were* a wicked old sinner and you *have been* saved by grace—but now you *are* a saint, a holy one! A saint who still sins, to be sure, but a saint nonetheless! Don't believe us? Then believe the apostle Paul! All through his letters, when he greets the believers, he calls them *saints*. Even the Corinthian church, whose behavior was often not very saintly, was greeted like that:

> To the church of God which is at Corinth, to those who have been sanctified in Christ Jesus, saints by calling, with all who in every place call on the name of our Lord Jesus Christ, their Lord and ours: Grace to you and peace from God our Father and the Lord Jesus Christ (1 Corinthians 1:2-3).

My religious background painted a wrong picture of a saint. When I (Joe) was growing up, to me a saint was a statue I prayed to, a superspiritual person who performed miracles and who was, years and years later, declared to be a "saint" by the Church. In other words, I knew I was not—and likely would never be—a saint. But in Christ, I am now St. Joseph! So the next time you're wearing a name tag, put a "St." in front of your name. (Just don't put it after your name or you become a street!)

A Decision to Make

If we believers in Christ are saints, then why is sin still a problem? After all, Romans 6:1-7 makes it clear that we are dead to sin and alive to God. But being dead to sin does not mean we are incapable of sinning—it means sin no longer holds tyrannical control over our lives. We can now choose righteousness instead of unrighteousness. As Ephesians 4:20-32 teaches, we must now choose to "lay aside" the old self and its practices and "put on" the new. As Christians we are now faced with just two choices every day: to walk according to the flesh (self-sufficiency without Christ's strength) or to walk by faith in the power of the Holy Spirit, doing things God's way (see Galatians 5:13-18).

In essence, though we have been rescued from the gutter, then adopted into God's royal family and given a whole new clean wardrobe, we still have a choice to make. We can get up in the morning, go to the closet, pull out and put on those new, sharp-looking garments…or we can put on those old, filthy rags lying in a heap on the floor. And sadly, sometimes we do just that. After all, though they look bad and smell bad and have nothing to do with our new identity, they are familiar, and we know how to act in them.

Such is the lure of sin. It promises a measure of pleasure and familiarity. And to be sure, it does require faith to take the first step, then continue to walk around, in the garments of righteousness we have in Christ. And faith can seem risky—until you truly get to know the One who holds your hand.

Therefore, we need to remind ourselves that the new covenant (New Testament) call to a righteous walk is based on Him and who we have now become in Him—new creations! As Paul wrote in Ephesians 4:1, "I, the prisoner of the Lord, implore you to walk in a manner worthy of the calling with which you have been called":

- It is the calling of the slave to sin who has been set free to be a slave to righteousness instead (Romans 6:20-22).

- It is the calling of the one rescued from the domain of darkness to now walk as a child of the light (Colossians 1:13; Ephesians 5:6-10).

- It is the calling of those who were dead in sin but who have been brought to life to walk in newness of life (Ephesians 2:1-5; Romans 6:4).

- It is the calling of the one who was once a helpless POW in the enemy's cruel concentration camp to fight the good fight as a good soldier of Christ Jesus (2 Timothy 2:3; 4:7).

As Paul again wrote so pointedly,

> When you were slaves of sin, you were free in regard to righteousness. Therefore what benefit were you then deriving from the things of which you are now ashamed? For the outcome of those things is death. But now having been freed from sin and enslaved to God, you derive your benefit, resulting in sanctification, and the outcome, eternal life (Romans 6:20-22).

Sin is a liar. It never delivers what it promises, and what it ends up delivering is a heart that becomes increasingly hard (Hebrews 3:12-13). When we give in to sin, we deny the reality of who we are and what we were made for in Christ—and in actuality, we declare civil war against our own bodies. First Peter 2:9-11 sums this up powerfully:

> You are a chosen race, a royal priesthood, a holy nation, a people for God's own possession, so that you may proclaim the excellencies of Him who has called you out of darkness into His marvelous light; for once you were not a people, but now you are the people of God; you had not received mercy, but now you have received mercy. Beloved, I urge you as aliens and strangers to abstain from fleshly lusts which wage war against your soul.

A Legacy to Share

When a man or woman becomes a marine, there is a long legacy of valiant warriors and courageous heroes in whose bootsteps the new Marine must follow. And he or she is proud to do it—having now been given the high honor and responsibility to guard the tradition of *semper fidelis* ("always faithful"), the U.S. Marine Corps motto.

To be an effective Marine, a person must jettison all that hinders. To be a good soldier in active service of the Lord Jesus Christ, a believer must disentangle himself or herself from civilian-thinking and civilian-living (see 2 Timothy 2:3-4).

In Hebrews 11 we have the chance to see on parade review, so to speak, a bit of the glory of such heroes of the faith as Abel, Enoch, Noah, Abraham, Isaac, Jacob, Joseph, Moses, Rahab, and others. No perfect ones there by any stretch of the imagination—but they were all ones who chose to walk with God in the midst of the toughest challenges.

We believe there are still places to fill in God's Hall of Faith. But if we want to be honored like these heroes, we must choose to walk like them. Hebrews 12:1-3 throws out the challenge:

> *Since we have so great a cloud of witnesses surrounding us [the men and women of Hebrews 11], let us also lay aside every encumbrance and the sin which so easily entangles us, and let us run with endurance the race set before us, fixing our eyes on Jesus, the author and perfecter of faith, who for the joy set before Him endured the cross, despising the shame, and has sat down at the right hand of the throne of God. For consider Him who has endured such hostility by sinners against Himself, so that you will not grow weary and lose heart.*

Dear heavenly Father, You found me when I was in a spiritual desert—a howling wasteland of wilderness—lost, hopeless and helpless, and without You in this world. You gathered me up, cared for me, and guarded me like the pupil of Your eye. You brought me into Your family, cleaned me up from the inside out, and gave me a new lease on life. You've given me a new start, a new heart, and Your very life within me. You have called me Your child! And so, today, I accept Your invitation to walk according to that calling as Your holy son (Your holy daughter). And I accept the challenge to throw off everything that would hinder my serving You as Your soldier. I will fix my eyes on You, Jesus, because it is in Your suffering, enduring, and victorious footsteps that I choose to follow. Amen.

For Further Scripture study
on your new identity in Christ:

Read and meditate on the truths of Ephesians 1.

Questions for reflection and discussion:

Many times, life in a tough world has resulted in "labels" slapped onto our hearts. They can be names designed to tear us down, like "stupid," "ugly," "evil," "inadequate"— or even things that once brought us a measure of pride, like "great athlete," "A-student," "can do anything he or she puts his or her mind to," and so on. As long as we see ourselves as we once were, in the flesh, we are hindered from walking in our new identity in Christ. Based on this chapter, how does God see you?

Sin can bring pleasure for a while, but what are sin's consequences?

How does knowing who you are in Christ provide motivation and encouragement to run away from temptation and sin and pursue righteousness?

What do you need to "lay aside" or "throw off" today that has encumbered you or entangled you, making it hard to run the Christian race and fight the spiritual battle?

3

Armed and Dangerous

The sun seemed to pause for a moment at the horizon before launching another scorching day in the tropics of Southeast Asia. It was one of those tranquil moments to get lost in, and my mind mercifully took a few-second vacation away from the intensity of life in a war zone. Snapping me back to reality, a voice from our mission's Command and Control helicopter crackled through the earphones in my flight helmet.

"Cu Chi Tower, Cu Chi Tower, this is Little Bear Six in the bear pit with seven slicks and two stingers in the hornets' nest for takeoff."

The air-traffic controller fired back instructions at a rapid pace, as there were literally scores of other pilots requesting taxiing and takeoff clearance to fly their missions. Whether it was reconnaissance, resupply, air support, medical evacuation (medevac), or combat assault, daybreak signaled another day to engage the enemy. Today our unit would fly another combat assault mission. We all came to a hover in flight formation as the tower operator confirmed, "Roger, Little Bear Six, you are cleared to go out runway 24. Contact air-traffic control and Cu Chi artillery before clearing the perimeter."

We moved to the active runway, ready to take off in flight formation. Training, precision, planning, and vigilance were essential, not only for flight safety and insertion of troops into the LZ, but for the overall success of the mission.

"Stingers" were gunship helicopters used for attack support. "Slicks" were UH-1H helicopters like mine, each loaded with a four-man crew: two pilots (such as I was) up front, our crew chief, and a door gunner, who was strapped into the rear of the chopper behind his M-60 machine gun. Space and weight limitations allowed us to carry only six infantrymen, since each was carrying upward of 80 to 90 pounds. of ammunition, water, and supplies.

Swiftly moving down the runway my fellow pilot and I each monitored three to four different radio frequencies at any given time. This was as difficult to master as flying the aircraft itself. During takeoff, the crew chief and door gunner (who sat on opposite sides) would let us know via intercom if we were getting dangerously close to others in our formation. There was also communication with other helicopters, including the gunships flying with us, and sometimes with F-4 bomber pilots moving in ahead of us to drop their napalm around the LZ, clearing the way for our landing.

As we gained altitude and airspeed, we all monitored Cu Chi's artillery frequency. There were artillery batteries placed at strategic locations around the base camp, which fired into our LZ and other targets. To fly in front of them was to risk being shot down by friendly fire. Once clear of the perimeter, Little Bear Six—the Command and Control helicopter identified by this call sign—which was flying higher and out in front of us, would direct our assault into the LZ.

Climbing quickly to 1500 feet, we were effectively out of range of small-arms fire. There were no cargo doors on our aircraft, and as the hundred-knot wind blew through our open troop compartment, it provided temporary relief from the oppressive jungle heat.

We were rapidly approaching our target. From high above, Little Bear Six ordered us to drop down to just above tree level. Everyone tensed up. There was no way of knowing what kind of situation we might encounter.

The artillery was already pounding the area with 105mm shells. On our flank was a forward air controller marking targets for the F-4

Phantom pilots, who flashed by us screaming upward after dropping their napalm loads. Helicopter gunships went into their racetrack pattern on either side of the formation, providing us with rocket and machine-gun cover fire around the perimeters of the LZ.

I gave the order to the door gunners to lay down suppressive fire into the tree line surrounding us. All of the pilots flared the noses of our birds in unison, carefully feeling for the ground below us. The infantrymen (or "grunts") weren't waiting for us to touch down. They had already spotted the muzzle flashes from the enemy's AK-47 automatic weapon fire. Men were screaming and guns firing. It was a "hot" LZ. The grunts jumped out both sides of the helicopter and moved quickly into combat formation to engage the enemy as we started to lift off and head for base.

Men had already been wounded, and the medics on the ground were doing everything they could to apply field dressings to stop the bleeding and prevent loss of life. Other soldiers who were unwounded leaned heavily into the firefight. A couple of our slicks who had just cleared the tree line stayed at low level, out of enemy sight. We made a quick 180 and headed back into the teeth of the battle to extract the wounded. It would take too long for the medevac choppers to arrive. We had to do it ourselves.

The gunships above were running low on fuel and ammunition and would soon need to return to base camp to rearm and refuel. Our slicks could return quickly with reinforcements if needed, or extract our troops if they were heavily outnumbered or when the battle was over.

The platoon commander on the ground called the artillery and air-support units to adjust their fire to the front of the assault. Maps of the area had to be read quickly and accurately. One small mistake could have resulted in dropping a shell into the middle of our own troops. Trust between infantrymen, artillery, and air support was vital as the radio operators coordinated the adjustment in weapons fire.

Soon both the artillery and air-support firepower were swishing safely overhead, exploding into the enemy's position.

To those in Washington, DC, and Hanoi, North Vietnam, this was just one of many combat assaults, but to those on the ground and those of us providing air support, the stakes were much higher. The battle had just begun and it was a life-or-death situation.

Were we ever anxious, nervous, or even afraid going into these battles? Of course we were, but we were compelled to do our job anyway. Courage is not the absence of fear; it is doing what is right and necessary even in the face of fear. Every time we went out on a mission, there was the possibility we might not return whole or even alive, but we did not and could not allow those thoughts to control us.

~

In the spiritual battles some of our brothers and sisters in Christ around the world experience, it *is* a life-or-death situation. In some countries imprisonments, beatings, torture, and even death await those who convert to Christianity or attempt to bring others to the faith.

In this nation, however (at least at the present time), the risks are not so great. When we share the gospel, we might experience someone sighing in boredom or rolling their eyeballs in contempt. We might experience shunning by a fellow employee or classmate, or even rejection from a family member or friend. Those occurrences are painful, no doubt about it, but they are certainly not life-threatening.

Unfortunately, most of us never get to the point of knowing how the other person might respond to the gospel because we lose the spiritual battle for our minds long before. The anxiety and nervousness and fear we experience in anticipation of sharing the good news steal our joy, kill our enthusiasm, and destroy our will to reach out. And sadly, instead of "running to the battle lines" like David did with Goliath (1 Samuel 17:22), we grab a snack and turn on the TV.

We Have Some Advantages

So we can win this battle for our minds, it is crucial to remember that, on the positive side of the ledger, we have God's powerful, state-of-the-art weaponry going for us. When, in Vietnam, our attack forces were headed out to a hostile and dangerous LZ, we knew what we had to do in order to accomplish the mission because we had been well-trained. Sometimes a large part of the believer's spiritual battle in this area can be won by getting some basic training. Organizations like Campus Crusade for Christ have trained hundreds of thousands of everyday Christians in personal evangelism. *Becoming a Contagious Christian* by Bill Hybels is another resource to equip God's people to spread the good news. Talk to one of your church leaders about your desire to get practical, relational training on how to share your faith. It's amazing how much boldness you can develop when you know what to do and are empowered by the Holy Spirit to do it!

Then, our forces were equipped with the best the U.S. Army had to offer at that time. As a chopper pilot I was equipped with an armored "chickenplate" that fit under the shoulder harness in my seat and protected my chest and abdomen. The seat itself was armored, protecting my back. I also carried a loaded firearm, which I used on occasion when under attack. We were not invulnerable by any stretch of the imagination, but with the technology to defend ourselves and the weapons to attack with precision and power—combined with good training—in our helicopters we *were* armed and dangerous.

Child of God, do you know that in Christ we are armed and dangerous, too? No, we don't fight with napalm or artillery shells, let alone nuclear weapons. But, when it comes to spiritual battle, God has outfitted us with spiritual weapons of great power. Consider these scriptures:

> *Though we live in the world, we do not wage war as the world does. The weapons we fight with are not the weapons of the world. On the contrary, they have divine power to demolish*

strongholds. We demolish arguments and every pretension that sets itself up against the knowledge of God, and we take captive every thought to make it obedient to Christ (2 Corinthians 10:3-5 NIV).

Our struggle is not against flesh and blood, but against the rulers, against the powers, against the world forces of this darkness, against the spiritual forces of wickedness in the heavenly places. Therefore, take up the full armor of God, so that you will be able to resist in the evil day, and having done everything, to stand firm. Stand firm, therefore, having girded your loins with truth, and having put on the breastplate of righteousness, and having shod your feet with the preparation of the gospel of peace; in addition to all, taking up the shield of faith with which you will be able to extinguish all the flaming arrows of the evil one. And take the helmet of salvation, and the sword of the Spirit, which is the word of God (Ephesians 6:12-17).

The night is almost gone, and the day is near. Therefore let us lay aside the deeds of darkness and put on the armor of light. Let us behave properly as in the day, not in carousing and drunkenness, not in sexual promiscuity and sensuality, not in strife and jealousy. But put on the Lord Jesus Christ, and make no provision for the flesh in regard to its lusts (Romans 13:12-14).

[In the midst of suffering and enduring, we battle] in purity, in knowledge, in patience, in kindness, in the Holy Spirit, in genuine love, in the word of truth, in the power of God; by the weapons of righteousness for the right hand and the left (2 Corinthians 6:6-7).

The Ultimate Reason to Fight

Whoever heard of fighting a war with things like kindness and patience? Well, it shouldn't surprise us if God's weapons are different than man's! One day during the reign of King Jehoshaphat of Judah, "a great multitude" came against the Israelites from Ammon, Moab, and Mount Seir (2 Chronicles 20:1-30). What weapons did God's people use in this battle?

First, the king and people proclaimed a fast and sought the Lord (verse 3). I doubt that you would find "Deprive the troops of food and call a prayer meeting" in any military strategy textbook, but that's what God told them to do.

Second, all the people, including the women and children, were gathered together as the king tried to figure out what to do (verse 13). Sure doesn't sound wise, does it—the leaders clueless and letting all the people know it? A surefire recipe for mass hysteria! But that was genuine humility on Jehoshaphat's part, and it pleased God.

Third, some guy from the crowd told the king what God was telling them to do, and the king did it. The strategy? Send out the choir and start praising God (verses 14-22). Unbelievable!

But it worked! Why? Because the people had sought the Lord and it was His strategy, not theirs. After the people began praising God, here were the results:

1. The enemy armies turned on each other and wiped each other out (verses 22-23).

2. When the armies of God's people peeked over the hill to see what had happened, there was not one enemy soldier left alive (verse 24).

3. Jehoshaphat and company spent the next three days gathering the goodies the enemy soldiers had brought with them (verse 25).

4. On the fourth day they had a big celebration and parade back to Jerusalem to proclaim the incredible things God had done (verses 26-28)!

5. All the neighboring armies were scared spitless of Israel, and peace came to the land *because God got the glory* (verses 29-30).

In a nutshell, all spiritual warfare is a battle for the glory of God. Dr. Timothy Warner explains this:

> Satan cannot compete at the level of glory. Any aspects about him which are or were glorious came from a reflected glory and not from any quality of his own. The glory of God, however, derives from qualities in His very nature and thus depends on no source higher or other than Himself. His creative and sustaining power evidenced in our universe and taken as a whole begins to define God's glory. At best Satan's acts are deceptive shows of power or counterfeits of God's mighty acts in order to impress and lead astray a people whose perceptions have been badly distorted by sin.[6]

The devil and his demons don't want God to look good, and they will try to defame His name by making you look bad. So, as you look at the battles you are facing—whether the strong temptation to do evil, the attacks of guilt, shame, fear, or anxiety of the enemy, or the deception of materialism and the love of stuff—ask the Lord to show you how to fight...*for His glory!*

God-Provided Armor

The following list of weapons from the Ephesians 6 passage mentioned on page 54 should help you get dressed for war. Remember, when you put on all the armor of God you *will* be able to resist in the evil day, and after you have done *everything* you will be able to stand (verse 13)!

- **Truth:** Fill your mind with the truth of God's Word and keep focused on things that are true, right, and pure (Philippians 4:8). Be open, honest, real, walking in the light (1 John 1:7). Have nothing to do with lying or deceiving. When you know the truth of what God really says, the truth will set you free from the deception of sin and Satan (John 8:32).

- **Righteousness:** Know who you are: the righteousness of God in Christ (2 Corinthians 5:21). There is no condemnation for those in Christ Jesus (Romans 8:1). Reject all accusing, guilt-producing, and shaming thoughts in your mind. If you sin, confess it and walk in God's forgiveness (1 John 1:9). Choose to walk in holiness each day, relying on the Holy Spirit's strength.

- **Peace:** You are at peace with God through faith in Jesus (Romans 5:1). Cast all anxiety on the Lord because He cares for you (1 Peter 5:7). Pray with thanksgiving about the things that worry you; God will give you His peace (Philippians 4:6-7). Step out in faith and bring the gospel of peace to people without Christ.

- **Faith:** Slanderous attacks on your reputation, threats against you or your family, illness, injury, times of mourning, injustices against you by employers or fellow employees, lawsuits, government intrusions, criminal acts against you, natural disasters, and so on, *can* be from the enemy—at the very least he will try to use them to discourage you or tempt you to cave in to fear. Stand firm in God's love and goodness and faithfulness. Claim the truths of Romans 8:28-39.

- **Salvation:** When life is a battle and the world seems crazy, the bottom line is that, in Christ, you belong to God. You have the mind of Christ, and as you walk with Him and cry out to Him in prayer, He will protect your mind. In a life-or-death situation, know that death has lost its sting and that physical death is simply a gateway to the loving, healing, forever arms of Jesus (1 Corinthians 15:54-58; 2 Corinthians 5:7-8).

- **The Word of God:** When besieged by the enemy through attacks of temptation, accusation, or deception, do what Jesus did: Quote an appropriate truth from Scripture with authority (Matthew 4:1-11). No lie can stand against the truth. Ask the Holy Spirit to "train your hands for battle" (Psalm 18:34) to use this devastating weapon. Make the Word of God your focus in preaching, teaching, encouraging, discipling, counseling, and advising (2 Timothy 4:1-5). Let your words be His word!

As you step out in faith and watch God come through, your faith and confidence in Him and in His using you will grow. And when you fail, you will experience His grace to sustain you and motivate you to continue the battle. And you will learn to be a good soldier of Christ Jesus.

One final word: When entering a battle zone in Vietnam, one of our greatest strengths was our confidence in *each other*. The commands to "put on the full armor of God" were not given to an individual. They were written to a church—a group of believers loving each other and battling for each other. True, each individual has the responsibility to personally choose truth, walk in righteousness, and so on, but we are not in this alone. We have each other.

Dear heavenly Father, You have said, "Do not be overcome by evil, but overcome evil with good" (Romans 12:21). Please empower me by the Holy Spirit to put on the full armor of God and use the weapons You've given me in Christ. I want to be well-trained in love, patience, kindness, humility, purity, praise and worship, prayer and fasting, truth, righteousness, peace, the proclamation of the gospel, faith, salvation, and Your Word so I can resist, stand firm, and fight the spiritual battles in and around me. Connect me with other like-minded brothers and sisters in Christ so we can lock arms and armor together. Thank You that since Jesus has already won the war, together we can win the battles—in Your kingdom, by Your power, and for Your glory. In Jesus' name, amen.

For further Scripture study
on God's battle plan for warfare:

In 2 Kings 18 and 19, read about how God exalted righteous King Hezekiah and how through the Word of God he was able to thwart a blistering attack of accusation by an enemy king.

Questions for reflection and discussion:

What principles of life and warfare can you harvest from 2 Timothy 2:1-13? Try to make a personal application to your life today.

Looking back over the context of 2 Corinthians 6:1-10, there seems to be a lot in Paul's life that looks like defeat and not victory. In light of this passage, what might be a good definition of "victory in spiritual battle" from God's point of view?

As you look at the many weapons of righteousness God has given us, which one or ones have you tended to neglect? By that neglect, what attacks of the enemy might you be most vulnerable to?

What can you do this week to more intentionally gather around yourself other Christians who can stand with you in spiritual battle?

4

The Unseen Hand

Much of the Vietnam War took place under cover of night because the enemy could hide behind the veil of darkness and not be spotted from the air as they pushed supplies and men along the Ho Chi Minh trail from Cambodia into Vietnam. In response to this, the U.S. Army sent out ambush patrols, hoping to catch enemy troops by surprise.

Every ambush patrol had a different radio frequency. Our six-man crew would check in with all of them at designated times as we flew high above their positions from a safe altitude. We were like a mother hen spreading her wings over her chicks in order to protect them. However, we needed to be careful how we communicated to them so as not to compromise their locations with too much radio chatter. Each soldier on the ground was typically hunkered down in a fox-hole that had been quickly dug after dark, once the patrols had reached their night positions.

Many times the enemy would send only a few soldiers down a trail or river, scouting out the strength of our resistance before moving in with their larger force. Once the position of our ambush patrols was compromised, the rest of the enemy forces would swarm in and try to overrun them.

This November night in 1969 was quieter than most. We were flying high above the battlefield, making our rounds over more than 25 ambush patrols scattered across rice paddies, jungle trails, and rivers. Partway through our surveillance watch, we returned to base camp for refueling. As we sat on the landing pad—our engine on and our rotor blades turning at flight idle position—an urgent call came in over the radio, desperate for help. The patrol was under heavy fire and needed to be resupplied; their ammunition was running low.

Hurriedly we finished refueling, took on supplies, and raced back out to reinforce our troops. As we approached their position, I could see they were being overrun. We landed a few feet from where they were engaged in an intense battle. There was no time to extract them, as we were now coming under heavy fire as well. Neither were our soldiers willing to leave. They wanted to finish off what the enemy had started.

We dropped off our supplies of ammunition and water, and took off again with a sense of urgency for more supplies and to request artillery fire and gunship support for this besieged unit. As we reached our cruising altitude of 3000 feet, we were halfway back to base camp, just over the Michelin Rubber Plantation.

Suddenly our engine quit.

Immediately we went into emergency procedures in an effort to restart. We worked feverishly but we were falling out of the sky like a rock. I turned on the landing light in preparation for a crash landing. I could see the tops of the trees through the chin bubble at my feet. They were racing up toward us at lightning speed. I paused and thought to myself that in the next few seconds we were all going to die.

As a young boy growing up in church, I had been taught that if you ever found yourself in a place of approaching death, you needed to pray a prayer of contrition to receive pardon for any unsettled business between yourself and God. As I sat in my seat waiting to crash into the trees below, I had no thought of my relationship to God.

But He was obviously thinking of me.

Instinctively I turned the radio frequency to the emergency channel and screamed out the universal distress call—"Mayday! Mayday! Mayday! This is Little Bear 21 going down over the Michelin Rubber Plantation!" All of this transpired in just a few seconds. There was little time to think.

Moments before impact where we would literally crash and burn, unexplainably the power came roaring back into our engines. It was as if God had stretched out His hand and caught us. Our helicopter came to a hover just a few feet above the treetops. We then limped back to base camp…alive.

We tried to explain to our superior officers what had happened, but they wouldn't believe us. There was no mechanical reason for what we had experienced. The engine and rotor blades had been pushed beyond all limits and the aircraft was basically shot. They ended up attributing the whole incident to "pilot error."

Years later, I shared this story with Kathy in the peace and safety of our family room. To our amazement, we realized that at the same time I had been going down that night in Vietnam, she had been working as a nurse in a hospital in our hometown, thousands of miles away. She was caring for an elderly nun who was dying of cancer. The sister asked Kathy if there was a special man in her life. Kathy told her that there was this boy she loved who was flying helicopters in Vietnam. Kathy and this dear lady prayed for me that God would watch over me and protect me.

That day the sister died, and that night my life was spared.

I don't understand all the mystery involved with the sovereign rule of God and the free will of man. Nor can I explain why an all-powerful, all-good God allows the existence of a world where good things happen to bad people, and bad things happen to good people. Neither can I fathom the incredible honor, privilege, and responsibility that God grants His people in prayer. Most of all, I have no answer as to why my life was spared while the lives of thousands of other men were not.

But I do know this: God calls His people to pray, and His hand is moved when we do so. And victory in spiritual battle hangs in the balance with the prayers of the saints.

James 5:16 says, "The effective prayer of a righteous man can accomplish much." The context of that promise is healing, but the implications are even broader. If the prayers of righteous people accomplish great things for the kingdom of God, what happens (or doesn't happen) when the saints do *not* pray?

Is it possible that a saint struggling with tormenting thoughts of worthlessness or suicide or panic attacks or with other spiritual–mental conflict is suffering needless pain in part because of a lack of prayer—both on the part of that saint as well as the body of Christ? In that same chapter, James also says,

> *Is anyone among you suffering? Then he must pray* (James 5:13).

In this verse, the primary responsibility for prayer is placed squarely on the shoulders of the one who is suffering. This is a critical point, for it is easy for a believer who is under spiritual attack to feel like a helpless victim. In Christ, that is simply not the case. We may be called to endure suffering, but we still "overwhelmingly conquer through Him who loved us" (Romans 8:37). There are responsibilities that the one who is being attacked must bear—to pray, to confess any and all sin, to renounce lies, to forgive all offenses, to resist the enemy in the authority of Christ.

But the fact remains that when we face times of intense spiritual conflict, our prayers alone may not be enough. We need the army of God to come to our aid through intercession. Even after itemizing the armor of God, the apostle Paul made it clear that we need to be covering one another in prayer. (There are even some Bible teachers who say that one of the main purposes for the armor of God is so we *can* pray.) Paul tells us,

> *With all prayer and petition pray at all times in the Spirit, and with this in view, be on the alert with all perseverance and petition for all the saints, and pray on my behalf, that utterance may be given to me in the opening of my mouth, to make known with boldness the mystery of the gospel* (Ephesians 6:18-19).

If the apostle Paul recognized his need for prayer—and called the saints in Ephesus to be on guard, praying with perseverance for him and for each other—then we do well to follow his lead.

Beyond that, the Lord Jesus Himself "would often slip away to the wilderness and pray" (Luke 5:16). And at His hour of most brutal spiritual conflict—in the Garden of Gethsemane—He took Peter, James, and John with Him and asked that they keep watch in prayer along with Him (Mark 13:33-38).

Prayer: Good Men Needed

Just in case your experience with prayer has left you with an insipid, bland taste in your mouth, let the words of J. Oswald Sanders in his book *Spiritual Leadership* stir your heart:

> Both our Lord and His bondslave Paul made it clear that true prayer is not pleasant, dreamy reverie. "All vital praying makes a drain on a man's vitality. True intercession is a sacrifice, a bleeding sacrifice," wrote J.H. Jowett. Jesus performed many mighty works without outward sign of strain, but of His praying it is recorded, "He offered up prayers and supplications with strong crying and tears" (Hebrews 5:7).
>
> How pale a reflection of Paul and Epaphras' striving and wrestlings are our pallid and languid intercessions! "Epaphras... laboring earnestly for you in his prayers," wrote Paul to the believers at Colossae (Colossians 4:12). And to the same group, "I would that ye knew what great conflict I have for you" (2:1 KJV). The word for "wrestling" and "conflict" is that from which our "agonize" is derived. It is used of a man toiling in his work until utterly weary (Colossians 1:29) or competing in the arena for the coveted prize (1 Corinthians 9:25). It describes the soldier battling for his life (1 Timothy 6:12) or a man struggling to deliver his friend from danger (John 18:36). From those and other considerations it is clear that true praying is a strenuous spiritual exercise that demands the utmost mental discipline and concentration.[7]

Years ago, Evelyn Christiansen wrote the book *What Happens When Women Pray.* It was important because it confirmed how, in many ways, the prayers of godly women have kept the church on its feet and in the battle for a long time. Without a doubt, the entire body of Christ owes an enormous debt to the intercessory prayer service of women. Both of us sure do!

But there is a fresh movement in the Spirit. Men are beginning to take leadership and stewardship of this vital work of prayer. The old idea that prayer is "soft work" best suited for women, children, and the elderly is finally beginning to die. (In fact, every church ought to hold a funeral for that lie from the pit of hell!) It would be a strong affirmation of the virile ministry of intercessory prayer if every pastor gathered the leaders of his congregation together and prayed that God would mark them out as intercessors for the kingdom…and then all those leaders in turn laid hands on the men of the church, crying for God to mark them out for that role as well.

What victories would be won in lives! What battles fought and won for marriages and families! What life, vitality, and energy, and fruitful, filled-by-the-Spirit preaching and service would be unleashed for the kingdom!

Is this just our "good idea"? Not at all! The apostle Paul, under the direction of God the Holy Spirit, urged his apprentice-pastor, Timothy, "I want the men in every place to pray, lifting up holy hands, without wrath and dissension" (1 Timothy 2:8). Men praying publicly has been God's idea from the beginning!

We feel that, too often, Christian men are spiritually intimidated by their wives and other women in the church. And so our response as men has been to gravitate toward areas in which we feel more competent, safer, and more secure—the world of working with our hands and minds rather than our hearts. Both are needed, but the greater need is for spiritual leaders waging war on their knees.

Leonard Ravenhill was right. In his book *Why Revival Tarries* he lamented,

Poverty-stricken as the Church is today in many things, she is most stricken here, in the place of prayer. We have many organizers, but few agonizers; many players and payers, few pray-ers; many singers, few clingers; lots of pastors, few wrestlers; many fears, few tears; much fashion, little passion; many interferers, few intercessors; many writers, but few fighters. Failing here, we fail everywhere.[8]

It would be unthinkable for the U.S. Army to replace the men on the front lines of combat with women. Should it not be equally unthinkable to, by default, leave the ministry of intercessory prayer to women alone? Don't get us wrong. We're not saying that women shouldn't pray. God forbid! The church needs the prayers of women now more than ever! What we are calling for, however, is this: that men shed this unbiblical notion that the responsibility for holding up the prayer banner in the church and in the home falls mainly on our sisters in Christ.

A Direct Assault

Have we forgotten something?

Prayer is not rear-echelon activity; prayer is front lines spiritual warfare. It is the ultimate weapon in our "struggle… against the rulers, against the authorities, against the powers of this dark world and against the spiritual forces of evil in the heavenly realms" (Ephesians 6:12). It is as S.D. Gordon says in *Quiet Talks on Prayer:* "Prayer is striking the winning blow at the concealed enemy. Service is gathering up the results of that blow among the people we see and touch." In a sense it would be correct to say that prayer is not simply a weapon we use; it is the battle. That is why persevering in prayer is so difficult for most of us.[9]

To pray that God's kingdom come and His will be done on earth as it is in heaven (Matthew 6:10) is an open declaration of war. When we pray in this way, we are asking for God's plans to be accomplished and for the defeat of all demonic schemes, designs, and strategies opposed against His plans. Prayer is a direct assault on the enemy of our souls, seeking to rescue spiritual POWs, bring home those who are AWOL, and provide vigorous "air cover" for troops engaged in battle.

The apostles had their priorities straight. When faced with the very legitimate need of some widows in the early church, they delegated the serving of food to Spirit-filled deacons while remaining steadfast in their call. "We will devote ourselves to prayer and to the ministry of the word" (Acts 6:4).

Notice their order of priority. Prayer first, preaching second. There are many ministers eager to fill the pulpit, but how many are even more zealous to fall on their knees? That's where the real power to rock the domain of darkness comes from—from prayer-saturated preaching!

After our Lord's resurrection, 120 men and women shut themselves up in a room and prayed for ten days. Then the fire of Pentecost fell, and Peter preached a three-minute sermon. Three thousand were saved! A terrible blow fell upon the domain of darkness! The church was literally born out of a prayer meeting, and its growth was sustained, in large part, through saints devoting themselves to prayer (Acts 2:42).

Growing as a Prayer Warrior

All of us periodically need fresh inspiration from the Lord in the area of prayer. Recently I (Rich) and my wife, Shirley, attended a marriage conference facilitated by Joe and Kathy. We came away with numerous action points, but many of them had to do with prayer.

We had become a bit lazy, not intentionally praying for each other and for our kids. Prayer had been relegated to a drowsy minute or two before dropping off to sleep—hardly the thing spiritual warfare is made of!

Shirley and I agreed together to pray for our kids each night after they get into bed and to pray for them before they go off to school.

And we decided to have a short devotional and prayer time together each day as well. Have we perfectly fulfilled this commitment yet? No, but we are moving in the right direction as the Lord reminds us and empowers us.

If the Lord is showing you that you need to kick up your prayer life a notch or two, trust that He will empower you to do it. But you have to step out in faith and begin. Will it feel awkward at first? Maybe, but do it anyway. Here are some suggestions that you might want to prayerfully consider. You can't do everything at once to grow in your prayer life, but you *can* do something now. The Lord will show you what He wants you to do.

- Read a book on prayer, such as *The Prayer Life* by Andrew Murray. If you're new to the arena of prayer, something basic and simple like *A Life of Prayer* by Paul Cedar or *Praying by the Power of the Spirit* by Dr. Neil Anderson will start you in the right direction.

- Attend your church's prayer meeting. Even if you're a little nervous about praying out loud, try a simple one-sentence prayer of thanking the Lord for something in your life. You'll find it is easier than you think, and your confidence in prayer will grow as you continue to step out in faith.

- If married, talk to your spouse about praying together for even five minutes a day. A great way to start is to have one of you read a psalm out loud and then pray about what that psalm says. Psalms 103, 139, and 145 are super starters. Then ask each other for one prayer request and pray out loud briefly for each other.

- If not married, you can implement the previous idea with a friend.

- If you have children, ask them if there's anything that has been bothering them lately. Has anything been frightening them, discouraging them, or making them worried or angry—even if it is just a thought in their minds. You may have a great opportunity to give some encouragement to them. Pray for the Lord's protection over them as they sleep and wake. (For more information on how the enemy attacks our children and how you can stand against those attacks, we encourage you to read *Spiritual Protection for Your Children* by Dr. Neil Anderson, and also see our discussion in this book's appendix.)

- If God has given you a desire to see those held captive by the world, flesh, and devil set free, we encourage you to pray aggressively for those you know who are bound. For locations for Freedom in Christ Ministries training in how to prayerfully walk a hurting brother or sister through the "Steps to Freedom in Christ," consult our Web site at www.ficm.org.

With perseverance and prayerful patience and encouragement from our spouses and friends, we can all grow strong in spirit and step up to the plate in prayer leadership. And we have the assurance from God's word that the Spirit helps our weakness, for we do not know how to pray as we should, but the Spirit Himself intercedes for us with groanings too deep for words; and He who searches the hearts knows what the mind of the Spirit is, because He intercedes for the saints according to the will of God (Romans 8:26-27).

Only God can make a prayer warrior. He is looking for a few good men...and women. Come on and enlist today!

Dear heavenly Father, You say in Your word that we are to rejoice always, pray without ceasing, and give thanks in everything. And you tell us to be devoted to prayer, keeping alert in it with an attitude of thanksgiving. I can't honestly say that I have done that as consistently as You desire. Thank You for forgiving me for the times I have neglected prayer and tried to live life or wage spiritual battle in my own strength or with my own human resources.

I now ask You to rekindle a fire of passion for You and for prayer in my heart. Open my eyes to the spiritual battles in and around me and teach me to wage war on my knees. Thank You for sending the Holy Spirit to be my mentor in prayer. I choose now to shed the old garments of worry, fretting, arguing, controlling, and leaning on my own understanding to solve problems. Instead I put on my new garments as a warrior in prayer. In Jesus' name I ask these things, amen.

(1 Thessalonians 5:16-18; Colossians 4:2)

For further Scripture study on prayer:

Eavesdrop on Jesus' prayer for Himself and His disciples in John 17.

Questions for reflection and discussion:

According to John 14:13-14, John 15:7, and 1 John 3:21-22, what are some of the requirements for answered prayer in our lives? What does it mean to "pray in Jesus' name"?

What are two major reasons for not getting what we want from God? (See James 4:1-3.)

According to 1 Timothy 2:1-4, for whom should we be praying?

From the following scriptures, what are some of the important things that we should be praying for one another? (Ephesians 1:15-23; 3:14-21; Philippians 1:9-11; Colossians 1:9-12; 2 Thessalonians 3:1-3)

5
Under Cover

The U.S. military base at Cu Chi was built on land that was flat and dry, in an area that had been used primarily for raising cattle and farming vegetables.

Directly northeast of our base camp were the deadly Ho Bo Woods and the infamous Iron Triangle. These were favorite hiding places for the enemy, and were staging grounds for assaults against Saigon. They were filled with tunnel and bunker complexes lined with booby traps and storage areas for the enemy. Not far to the north was War Zone C, a triple canopy jungle that many believed was the command center for all Vietcong operations. To the south, the tranquil Oriental River flowed, serving as a supply line between VC bases.

Despite its precarious position, it never ceased to amaze me how much safer I felt when I was returning to base camp after any mission I flew. It was the closest thing to home I had during my tour of duty in Vietnam. Once I crossed the perimeter into the camp, parked my helicopter in its bunker, and shut the engine down, I thought everything would be all right.

But many nights we would receive rocket and mortar fire from outside the perimeter. Once the first rounds began to impact the barracks, the flight line where our aircraft were parked, and the fuel and ammunition depots, sirens would go off and we'd run to the bunkers just outside our "hootches."

"Hootch" was a term of endearment for the makeshift barracks where we slept. They were surrounded by sandbags designed to keep shrapnel from those incoming rounds from wounding or killing us. Despite these efforts at guarding us from harm, the barracks were not sufficient to withstand direct hits. On the other hand, the underground bunkers outside our barracks could withstand anything the enemy might throw at us.

⌐⌐

For the child of God, safety and security is not found in the buildings where we worship or even in the houses in which we dwell. As a matter of fact, these places often are the primary targets and focuses of the enemy's attacks. The only true sanctuary for the child of God is *in Christ,* living life under cover…*His* cover.

King David was more skilled and experienced in battle than most of us ever will be or ever care to be. In the following verses from Psalm 18, it is evident where his security really lay:

> *I love You, O LORD, my strength. The LORD is my rock and my fortress and my deliverer, my God, my rock, in whom I take refuge; my shield and the horn of my salvation, my stronghold. I call upon the LORD, who is worthy to be praised, and I am saved from my enemies…*
>
> *The LORD my God illumines my darkness. For by You I can run upon a troop; and by my God I can leap over a wall. As for God, His way is blameless; the word of the LORD is tried; He is a shield to all who take refuge in Him, for who is God, but the LORD? And who is a rock, except our God…?* (Psalm 18:1-3,28-31).

Another psalmist vividly pictured that same security in God:

> *He who dwells in the shelter of the Most High will abide in the shadow of the Almighty. I will say to the LORD, "My refuge and my fortress, my God, in whom I trust!" For it is He who delivers you from the snare of the trapper and from the deadly*

pestilence. He will cover you with His pinions, and under His wings you may seek refuge; His faithfulness is a shield and bulwark. You will not be afraid of the terror by night, or of the arrow that flies by day (Psalm 91:1-5).

Finding Safety

I (Rich) and my wife, Shirley, were speaking and counseling people at a summer Bible conference in Pennsylvania about six years ago. The group was very responsive to the message of freedom, and momentum grew as our ten days there progressed. We were excited about the good teaching our young children were getting as well.

Housing for the conference was tight, but we crammed all five of us (our whole family at that time) into one bedroom in a house on the camp property. As we were turning out the lights one night, Michelle, our then seven-year-old, piped up, "Daddy, I've got an imaginary friend. Her name is Becca. She's a little orphan girl and she lives in this old house. She was waiting for us and she wants to sleep with me tonight and go home and live with our family."

Understanding that the enemy is a clever deceiver and that he often masquerades as a harmless or even beneficial being, I immediately went on alert. My surprise quickly turned to fiery anger as I realized and thought about the evil designs this demon had on my daughter.

We recognize, of course, that many children have great imaginations and sometimes they can pretend that stuffed animals and other things talk to them. Much of that is harmless play. But this was totally different. Michelle had not created this being with her imagination. This was an entity that had taken the initiative to approach my daughter—not visually, but speaking into her mind—and had invited itself into her life. It was neither imaginary nor a friend.

Realizing the danger involved, I asked the Lord what to do. Because of Michelle's relationship with Christ and the background she already had in understanding spiritual warfare, I decided to take a direct

approach. Ever since Michelle was three years of age, I had taught her—
and she had understood—that Jesus was stronger than the bad angels.

"Sweetheart, sometimes bad angels get dressed up in costumes and
pretend to be something they are not. This is not a little orphan girl,
it is a demon. And you are going to have to tell it to go away and not
come back." Steam might have been coming out my ears but at least
my voice was calm!

"Okay, Daddy."

Fortunately Michelle did just that and "Becca" hit the road. Six
weeks later I checked to make sure it had not returned. I was con-
cerned that it would try to lure Michelle into keeping their "friendship" a secret. She assured me that "Becca" was history. Michelle has
never been approached in that way again.

Having won that victory, however, I had to ask the Lord why
Michelle had been vulnerable to such an attack. The answer came
swiftly. Shirley and I had become complacent while at the Bible conference. Surrounded by Christian people, in an environment where
real renewal was taking place, we had let down our guard as parents
and not prayed for protection for our family as we should. In our
deceived disobedience to God, our children had come out from under
the cover of God's protection, which was designed to come through
the spiritual authority of their dad and mom.

Our response? To immediately repent of our sin and begin praying
in earnest for our children again.

Proverbs 14:26 tells us that "in the fear of the LORD there is strong
confidence, and his children will have refuge." Shirley and I learned
that truth the hard way.

The Strength of Being Under Authority

The whole concept of submission to God's authority and human
authority doesn't, in general, sit very well with our independent, self-
reliant American spirit. We think very little—even in the church—

about fudging a bit on our taxes, using company time or office equipment and supplies for personal purposes, treating speed limits as speed suggestions, listening to and then quickly forgetting the Sunday sermon, and so on.

We need to realize that the whole strategy of waging and winning spiritual battle in the kingdom of God stands or falls on the question of *authority*. And the privilege of exercising spiritual authority is granted only to those who operate *under* spiritual authority.

Those in the military naturally understand this concept of authority better than civilians. And even though I (Joe) did not grasp the principles of spiritual warfare illustrated during our missions in Vietnam at the time, I can see them now.

For example, though I was well-trained to fly and was experienced in flying helicopters, I never took off on my own. I was always involved in a mission that was designed and coordinated by those higher up the chain of command. Pilots like myself were given orders by the Command and Control helicopter. In spiritual battle, God Himself designs the warfare strategies and assigns us our missions. We learn to listen to Him and submit to His authority in dependent prayer.

When we were flying, oftentimes we couldn't see where we were going, and so we had to rely on the tower operator, Cu Chi radar, and other radio communications coming in to us. It would have been foolish—and potentially fatal—for us to refuse their guidance. Likewise, when we launch out by faith into a mission the Lord gives us to accomplish, we don't know what to do. We may think we do, but we really don't. We are operating in unknown territory, and so the Lord has provided His Holy Spirit to lead us. In fact, that is a truth in Scripture, which says, "All who are being led by the Spirit of God, these are sons of God" (Romans 8:14).

The missions we flew were successful only to the degree that we obeyed our leaders and did our jobs in accordance with the training we'd received. That's how the military has always operated. And that is the way things work in the spiritual world as well.

Jesus and Authority

In Luke 7, the story is told of a centurion (a soldier in charge of 100 men) in the town of Capernaum who had a very sick slave. This centurion, though a Roman, was highly respected by the Jews and loved the nation of Israel. He had even built the local synagogue (verses 1-5).

As Jesus headed toward the soldier's house, friends of the centurion intercepted Him and gave Jesus a message from the man:

> "*Lord, do not trouble Yourself further, for I am not worthy for You to come under my roof; for this reason I did not even consider myself worthy to come to You, but just say the word, and my servant will be healed. For I also am a man placed under authority, with soldiers under me; and I say to this one, 'Go!' and he goes, and to another, 'Come!' and he comes, and to my slave, 'Do this!' and he does it*" (verses 6-8).

Jesus was astonished at this Gentile soldier's faith and announced to the crowd, "I say to you, not even in Israel have I found such great faith" (verse 9).

What was it about this man's faith that caused Jesus to be so amazed? Certainly a large part of it was that the soldier recognized that Jesus had the capacity to heal from far away as well as He could in person. But there is another component to it. The centurion recognized that Jesus, like himself, was "also a man placed under authority." Not a man *with* authority (though Jesus was certainly that), but a man *under* authority.

In John 5:19 (and John 5:30 and elsewhere), Jesus stated categorically that He operated totally under the authority of God the Father, which John recorded:

> *Jesus answered and was saying to them, "Truly, truly, I say to you, the Son can do nothing of Himself unless it is something*

*He sees the Father doing; for whatever the Father does, these
things the Son also does in like manner."*

During Jesus' 40 days of fasting in the wilderness, each of the devil's
temptations was an attempt to get Him to act apart from submission
to the Father's authority. First, the devil urged Jesus to zap a rock and
turn it into a loaf of bread in order to alleviate his body's intense
hunger. He then encouraged Him to take His own path to authority
over the nations and become king the fast and easy way by worship-
ping the devil. And finally, Satan encouraged Him to wow the crowds
by taking a flying leap off the temple, by His act demanding of God
to provide a huge angelic cushion to break His fall (see Luke 4:1-13).

But Jesus would have none of it. He didn't enter into discussion.
He didn't try to match wits with the devil. He didn't try to beat him
in an argument. Filled with the Holy Spirit, Jesus stood under the
authority of the Father and three times quoted the authoritative Word
of God. And the devil took off. He had to, because the liar cannot stand
against the Truth.

Why do you think that Jesus, the Son of God—and God Himself—
chose to live life on earth without one shred of self-reliance? He was
showing us the way we can live and are to live in respect to our heavenly Father.

Where Do You Stand?

Where do you stand today in relation to the Father's authority in
your life? Where does your heart stand in regard to the human authorities He has placed over you? Knowing how easy it is to let this matter
of submission slide, please—for the sake of your own life, family, and
church—prayerfully look over the following scriptures:

*He gives a greater grace. Therefore it says, "God is opposed to
the proud, but gives grace to the humble." Submit therefore to
God. Resist the devil and he will flee from you* (James 4:6-7).

You younger men, likewise, be subject to your elders; and all of you, clothe yourselves with humility toward one another, for God is opposed to the proud, but gives grace to the humble. Therefore humble yourselves under the mighty hand of God, that He may exalt you at the proper time (1 Peter 5:5-6).

Honor your father and mother (which is the first commandment with a promise), so that it may be well with you, and that you may live long on the earth (Ephesians 6:2-3).

Wives, be subject to your own husbands, as to the Lord. For the husband is the head of the wife, as Christ also is the head of the church, He Himself being the Savior of the body. But as the church is subject to Christ, also the wives ought to be to their husbands in everything. Husbands, love your wives, just as Christ also loved the church and gave Himself up for her (Ephesians 5:22-25).

Every person is to be in subjection to the governing authorities. For there is no authority except from God, and those which exist are established by God. Therefore whoever resists authority has opposed the ordinance of God; and they who have opposed will receive condemnation upon themselves…Therefore it is necessary to be in subjection, not only because of wrath, but also for conscience' sake. For because of this you also pay taxes, for rulers are servants of God, devoting themselves to this very thing. Render to all what is due them; tax to whom tax is due; custom to whom custom; fear to whom fear; honor to whom honor (Romans 13:1-2,5-7).

Act as free men, and do not use your freedom as a covering for evil, but use it as bondslaves of God. Honor all people, love the brotherhood, fear God, honor the king. Servants, be submissive to your masters with all respect, not only to those who are good and gentle, but also to those who are unreasonable. For this finds favor, if for the sake of conscience toward God a person bears up under sorrows when suffering unjustly (1 Peter 2:16-19).

Slaves, in all things obey those who are your masters on earth, not with external service, as those who merely please men, but

> *with sincerity of heart, fearing the Lord. Whatever you do, do*
> *your work heartily, as for the Lord rather than for men, knowing*
> *that from the Lord you will receive the reward of the inheritance.*
> *It is the Lord Christ whom you serve. For he who does wrong*
> *will receive the consequences of the wrong which he has done,*
> *and that without partiality* (Colossians 3:22-25).

> *Obey your leaders and submit to them, for they keep watch over*
> *your souls as those who will give an account. Let them do this*
> *with joy and not with grief, for this would be unprofitable for*
> *you* (Hebrews 13:17).

You may feel a bit bombarded by all these scriptures. We did that for a reason. The mentality of self-sufficiency, self-determination, self-reliance, self-promotion, and selfish ambition is so rampant in our national psyche (and tragically, in the church as well) that we felt like we needed to launch a bit of a scriptural artillery barrage.

If you have been living life on the ragged edge of independence and isolation, we earnestly urge you to come under the protective care of God and the authorities He has placed over you. That is the only place of spiritual safety available to you.

If you have already been living in humility and submission, we commend you and encourage you to continue to walk in this way. By so doing you are well on your way to winning the spiritual battles in your life.

Please understand what we are saying, however. Submission does not mean being a doormat. It does not mean being afraid to state your opinion or express your disagreement to an authority figure. Rather, it is an attitude of trust and dependence upon God Himself. It is believing that He will work in and through those imperfect authorities in your life—in the home, in the marketplace, in the church, and in the community. And that attitude of trust and dependence results in your respectfully expressing yourself while humbly submitting and obeying, even if what you are being asked to do is not your preference.

In those instances when human authorities abuse the power that they have, though, it is right and just for those under authority to seek help from a higher authority. A verbally abusive coach should be reported to the athletic director. A Sunday school teacher who is teaching error should be reported to the Sunday school superintendent. A man who is physically or sexually abusing his wife and kids should be reported to the local authorities. A church leader who misuses his authority over the congregation should be held accountable by the church or denominational leadership. A police officer who brutally beats a suspect must be held accountable by a court of law. A congressman who refuses to act in the best interests of the constituency he represents should be voted out of office. And so on.

And in those moments when human authorities at the highest level fail to do what is right and instead try to force us to do what is wrong or not do what is right, then we must obey God rather than men (see Acts 4:18-20).

The Cosmic Consequences of Submission

In the realm of spiritual warfare, the matter of submission becomes an issue of cosmic consequences. As we have noted, James 4:7 says, "Submit therefore to God. Resist the devil and he will flee from you." What is going to happen if you don't first submit to God's authority, including the human authorities over you? What will happen if you try to resist the devil when you are not under that protective authority-shield? He will certainly not flee and in fact, may turn and cause serious damage to you and your loved ones.

John Paul Jackson, in his book *Needless Casualties of War,* warns believers against engaging in presumptuous spiritual battle. By this he means individuals or groups of people who verbally confront high-level powers of darkness without an assignment from God and a clear covering of protection from the church. This sort of activity can be born of impatience[10] or pride. Spiritual "loose cannons" (those operating as self-proclaimed "apostles" or "prophets" but refusing to come under wise, healthy, balanced spiritual authority) present a grave danger to themselves and others.

Jackson uses a couple of war movies to illustrate spiritual truth, providing a wise admonition:

> In the movie *Navy Seals,* there was a young naval officer who was ordered by his commanding officer to carry out a stealth infiltration/exfiltration operation. Although the officer was gifted, he constantly endangered missions by taking unecessary gambles. On one mission, everything was going like clockwork until the young officer ran out from under cover and fired on the enemy, although he had prior orders *not* to do so. Consequently, he endangered the mission and the people around him. As a result, a team member died in a deadly firefight. A similar loss of judgment is illustrated in the movie *Saving Private Ryan.* Tom Hanks plays a Ranger infantry captain who is ordered to find Private Ryan and escort him to safety. In one scene, Hanks' character has a tragic loss of judgment. His judgment is clouded not because of thrill-seeking or ego gratification but because of battle fatigue. He orders his unit into an unnecessary skirmish that has little to do with his mission. They succeed, but at a great cost—they lose valuable team members.[11]

It is easy to get intoxicated with the notion that we are on the winning side and to begin to view ourselves as spiritual SWAT team members who are invincible in whatever we set our minds to do. Jesus warned against such potentially disastrous spiritual giddiness when He told His disciples,

> *Behold, I have given you authority to tread on serpents and scorpions, and over all the power of the enemy, and nothing will injure you. Nevertheless do not rejoice in this, that the spirits*

are subject to you, but rejoice that your names are recorded in
heaven (Luke 10:19-20).

As the disciples went out to preach the gospel and heal the sick, they were confronted by the powers of darkness, and so also will we be. In the midst of their ministry to hurting and needy people, they dispatched the demons that were harassing those people, and so also can we. Where believers in Christ have suffered harm, however, is by venturing into realms of spiritual battle where even angels would fear to tread.

I remember a time when I (Rich) was in Beijing, China. Walking through Tiananmen Square, I spotted two huge, demonic-looking lion statues guarding the gate into the Imperial City and noticed the immense photo of Mao Tse-Tung hanging from the gate's wall. I was stirred in my spirit. Knowing a little about the oppressive treatment of followers of Christ by the Communist Chinese regime, I felt like I should do something about it.

What I should have done was ask God how to pray for the leaders of China, according to 1 Timothy 2:1-4:

> *I urge, then, first of all, that requests, prayers, intercession and*
> *thanksgiving be made for everyone—for kings and all those in*
> *authority, that we may live peaceful and quiet lives in all god-*
> *liness and holiness. This is good, and pleases God our Savior,*
> *who wants all men to be saved and to come to a knowledge of*
> *the truth* (NIV).

What I actually did instead was to verbally (out loud) demand that the principalities and powers holding China in their oppressive clutches would let go and that the "Bamboo Curtain" would fall.

Had God called me to go to China for such a prayer assignment? No. Was this action of mine born out of a lot of seeking God's advice and praying and fasting for spiritual discernment? No. Was it conducted under the informed, watchful, and supportive care of my home church?

No. Was it done at all in concert with other believers in China? Not at all. It was simply my fleshly attempt to "do something for God that would make me look really spiritual" if something actually happened.

John Paul Jackson would call such arrogant, impulsive, and presumptuous behavior "throwing hatchets at the moon." Futile, ineffective—and potentially very dangerous.

I do not mean that last statement at all lightly. Jackson has, in fact, encountered numerous cases of intercessors succumbing to devastating illnesses and experiencing heart-rending family tragedies as a result of their presumptuous praying. He has also seen these terrible afflictions reversed when the intercessors confessed and repented of their presumption.

A Strategy for Transformation

How then should believers in Christ endeavor to see the "spiritual DNA" of a nation (or a church, or even a family) changed? We would like to suggest several key elements for such a strategy of transformation.

Before we do this, however, we want to acknowledge that sometimes God does allow us to be in a situation where we must battle for this kind of change largely alone. We want to encourage those of you who are doing this. Don't give up, and don't give in to discouragement. Galatians 6:9 urges and promises, "Let us not become weary in doing good, for at the proper time we will reap a harvest if we do not give up" (NIV). Continue to ask the Lord to bring along like-minded people who will join with you in your prayers. Stay close to the Lord, and keep your heart gentle and humble toward those in authority over you, even if they remain resistant or even hostile to change.

There is great power unleashed through individual prayer. The apostle James, after speaking about the prophet Elijah, reminds us that "the prayer of a righteous man is powerful and effective" (James 5:16 NIV). Elijah accomplished great things for God in prayer because he was operating in a God-given calling that required him to be by himself much of the time. (Beware, however, of a spiritual "Lone Ranger" mentality—and always welcome others the Lord sends your way.)

In the case of a family, Scripture provides special encouragement for those longing to see righteousness reign in their homes, even when other family members are not believers:

> *The unbelieving husband has been sanctified through his wife, and the unbelieving wife has been sanctified through her believing husband. Otherwise your children would be unclean, but as it is, they are holy* (1 Corinthians 7:14 NIV).

Having said all that, we firmly believe there is greater spiritual power and authority released when God's people are operating in unity. Jesus indicated this would be so in His prayer in John 17:23. He prayed, "May they [God's people] be brought to complete unity to let the world know that you sent me and have loved them even as you have loved me" (NIV).

Something powerful is unleashed in the spiritual realm when God's people are unified. And something is sadly hindered when they are not. With that in mind, here are what we believe are the key elements needed to see true spiritual transformation occur:

- God is attracted to *humility.* He pours out His grace upon humble people who know and live in deep dependence upon Christ and who see their desperate need for one another (James 4:6-7).

- True humility comes out of *brokenness and deep repentance from sin*—including the sin of believing that you or your church or your denomination does not really need anyone else to fully accomplish the will of God. As Paul wrote, "The eye cannot say to the hand, 'I don't need you!'" (1 Corinthians 12:21 NIV). This brokenness will be painful but will pave the way to a deeper intimacy with Christ. James 4:8-10 says (and note that this is written to a group of people, not an individual),

Come near to God and he will come near to you. Wash your hands, you sinners, and purify your hearts, you double-minded. Grieve, mourn and wail. Change your laughter to mourning and your joy to gloom. Humble yourselves before the Lord, and he will lift you up (NIV).

- You can count on God placing His finger on the need for *forgiveness and reconciliation* as part of the process of building unity. God is very interested in hearing our prayers for transforming the unbelieving person or community, but He will never bypass His people resolving their personal conflicts with one another, as the following Scriptures indicate:

  When you stand praying, if you hold anything against anyone, forgive him, so that your Father in heaven may forgive you your sins (Mark 11:25 NIV).

  If you are offering your gift at the altar and there remember that your brother has something against you, leave your gift there in front of the altar. First go and be reconciled to your brother; then come and offer your gift (Matthew 5:23-24 NIV).

A battle plan for spiritual warfare—a mighty weapon of mass destruction to the domain of darkness, and a mighty force for mass reconstruction of the kingdom of God that will give glory to Him—will always be birthed out of brokenness, repentance, forgiveness, and humility. And it will then be revealed in unified prayer and carried out in unified action in the power of the Holy Spirit.

These great rebuildings will come when God's people are walking in freedom—*together*—as Isaiah predicted:

The Spirit of the Lord GOD is upon me, because the LORD has anointed me to bring good news to the afflicted; He has sent me to bind up the brokenhearted, to proclaim liberty to captives and freedom to prisoners; to proclaim the favorable year of the LORD and the day of vengeance of our God; to comfort all who mourn, to grant those who mourn in Zion, giving them a garland instead of ashes, the oil of gladness instead of mourning, the mantle of praise instead of a spirit of fainting. So they will be called oaks of righteousness, the planting of the LORD, that He may be glorified.

Then they will rebuild the ancient ruins, they will raise up the former devastations; and they will repair the ruined cities, the desolations of many generations (Isaiah 61:1-4).

> *Dear heavenly Father, I recognize that humility and submission to authority is not only Your will—and therefore good, acceptable, and perfect—but it is the way Jesus Himself walked. Please forgive me for the times I have foolishly believed I could do whatever I felt was right and that somehow I would be protected. Thank You that You have forgiven me. Forbid it, Lord, that I should ever put You to the test again. I now run into the strong tower that is Your name and realize that, in seeking to walk in humility, submission, and dependence on You, I will be safe. I also acknowledge that I desperately need the body of Christ. Knit my heart together with other believers so that corporately we can discern Your mind and accomplish Your purposes. In the gentle and humble name of Jesus, I pray. Amen.*

For further Scripture study
on the crucial requirement of humility and submission:

We encourage you to sit down and prayerfully read through 1 Peter. The book is very short and it won't take long. If time is a problem, then focus on chapter two, three, or five.

Questions for reflection and discussion:

Think about your life in terms of pride or humility. Is it hard for you to admit you are wrong? Do you tend to think you have no needs? Have you tended to view yourself as superior to others for any reason? Do you find it easier to help and serve others rather than accepting help and service from them? Talk to the Lord about these things and ask Him to build deep, genuine humility in your life.

In John 15, Jesus teaches that our relationship to Him is like that of branches to a vine. Go ahead and read that chapter. What message on humility and dependence is the Lord bringing to your heart through this passage?

Have you had a track record of rebelling against authority? Prayerfully think back to your relationship with parents, teachers, coaches, employers, state and federal laws, government officials, and church leaders. Is the Lord putting His finger on a rebellious spirit? If so, open your heart to Him and confess the actions and attitudes He brings to mind.

Come up with a definition of "submission" to authority. Word it in such a way that it is in accordance with the scriptures in this chapter. Write it so that you view it as a positive, protective principle, rather than a restrictive, suffocating burden.

6
Dirty Tricks

If you were the enemy, what would you do to take out the forces opposed to you? Wouldn't you hit them at their weakest, most vulnerable point? Wouldn't you try to avoid detection, sneak past their defenses, create confusion, and strike from within their own perimeter—at the place where they least expected it?

In Vietnam, even though our enemy was massively overmatched by American firepower, the North Vietnamese Army (NVA) and Vietcong (VC) were masters at guerrilla warfare, and they used every trick and strategy at their disposal. Our soldiers were trained in conventional warfare, and fighting an enemy we could not see was frustrating at best and deadly at worst.

In the last chapter I briefly mentioned how we had to move from our barracks and seek cover in bunkers when incoming artillery fire hit our base. When I arrived at Cu Chi base in September 1969, I literally had a rude awakening on just my third night there. What happened that night was scary enough—the reason for that incident (and many others like it) still sends chills up my spine to this day.

I was trying to get some sleep in the hot, mosquito-and-cockroach-infested hootch to which I had been assigned with the other pilots from my unit. I soon fell into a very deep sleep. I hadn't had much sleep since leaving the States and getting settled into this war zone, and so I was dog-tired.

Suddenly I woke up to the sounds of explosions going off all around me. As I sat up, I was sprayed with dirt and sand coming through the screens above my head—over the sandbags piled up to prevent shrapnel from penetrating the thin, screened-in walls built around our cots. Looking around, I saw that everyone else in our makeshift shelter had already vacated the premises for the underground bunkers outside.

Having never experienced incoming rocket and mortar fire before, I was disoriented and didn't know what to do. I felt like a fool, being the last one to stumble into the heavily fortified bunker out back. The rest of the pilots were already sitting around this damp, dingy hole in the ground in their OD green underwear, unstrapped combat helmets hanging around their heads, drinking beer. They laughed heartily as they watched the "new guy" barely escaping death come tumbling onto the dirt floor with a look of fear in his eyes.

I understood right then and there that I could never afford to sleep that deeply again. From that night on, and for many years after, I never would.

I soon found out that this was typical at Cu Chi. On many nights we could receive upward of 60 to 70 rounds of incoming fire. The NVA and VC were using one of their favorite tactics against large military installations such as ours. Their purpose was to steal our sense of safety and security, kill us, and destroy our military assets. They wanted us to know they could attack us anytime they desired, thus forcing us to use our sizeable resources in defending the base camp rather than in launching assaults against them. The result was a serious deterioration of morale because we felt helpless to defend ourselves. We never knew, day or night, when these enemy missiles might come slamming down on top of us or around us. It was never safe to let our guard down.

Hidden Dangers

Why was the enemy able to launch such consistent, devastating attacks on us inside the barbed-wired fortress of Cu Chi? Most soldiers thought it was because of VC informers who came in from the surrounding villages and worked there. But that was not the main reason.

An account of a 1966 operation designed to discover the military and political headquarters of the VC's Fourth Military region (just north of Cu Chi) shows that the mystery surrounding our area had been baffling the U.S. Army for years:

> As the operation progressed, the Americans came under VC sniper fire and engaged in small firefights. However, as the…[soldiers] approached the areas where their adversaries apparently were, there was no trace of them. The days progressed and the American casualties began to mount, but the frustrated soldiers were unable to engage the enemy and could only find some foxholes, trenches, and large caches of rice. Little did they know that the Vietcong were always only a few yards away.[12]

The reason this military operation failed to effectively engage the enemy was the same reason our base at Cu Chi came under such elusive, disturbing attack. No one knew it at the time, but Cu Chi had been built over an elaborate tunnel system constructed in the 1940s during Vietnam's war for independence from France. This tunnel complex had been expanded considerably in the 1960s so that it stretched 130 miles or more from the border of Cambodia to Saigon. It provided the enemy with a totally secret means of moving thousands of troops and their supplies into position to advance or retreat. And it provided the perfect cover for small bands of saboteurs, as the following account describes:

> When the American 25th Infantry Division first arrived in 1966, an enterprising Viet Cong called Huynh Van Co hid with two comrades underneath the [Cu Chi] camp for a week, emerging at night to wreak havoc and steal food. The newly arrived 25th were baffled by the attacks, assuming that mortar fire was coming in from outside their perimeter. But (in the

words of one general) they had bivouac'd on a volcano. After causing psychological damage out of all proportion to its military importance, Huynh Van Co and the others withdrew to the "belt" of tunnels surrounding the base. Neither they nor their tunnel were ever detected.[13]

A Network of Deception

This often three-tiered underground network of tunnels reached from the surface down to 30 or more feet deep. It included wells, airshafts, war rooms, mess halls, infirmaries, sleeping quarters, and storage depots, as well as staging points from which to attack. Remarkably, even training sites were located in the brutally hot, humid, and disease-infested environment under the earth. The ground consisted mainly of laterite, and when dry, this reddish-brown clay became hard as rock—perfect tunneling material.

The entrances to these tunnels were extremely well-hidden and often very well-guarded. If unwary, any one of our soldiers could step into punji pits with bamboo spikes smeared with dung. These poisoned stakes pierced the boot and foot, causing painful, debilitating infections. Worse yet was the terrible psychological effect on our troops. Even if a soldier had never encountered a punji pit, the mere thought that he *might* was enough to make him hesitate at each step.[14] Further, booby traps of explosives were often set around the tunnel entrances so that anyone attempting to follow the enemy would be maimed or killed.

Inside the tunnels, other explosive booby traps were set, as were trip wires that would release scorpions or poisonous snakes. Since the passages were purposely constructed with varying dips and turns ranging from 60 to 120 degrees, our soldiers never knew what waited for them around the next bend. Sometimes the Vietcong would wait in a dark chamber for an unsuspecting American to enter. Then, once the soldier peered into the aperture, the VC would garrote him or slit his throat.[15]

Although most of us would not have been caught dead in one of these tunnels, a very special breed of soldier (both South Vietnamese and American) was developed to fight an underground war to root out the enemy. These men came to be known as "tunnel rats." Armed with only a flashlight, handgun, and knife, these extraordinary, brave men became an elite group in Vietnam. Captain Herbert Thornton, the "father of the tunnel rats," commented on the unusual courage and temperament required to fight such a war:

> It took a special kind of being. He had to have an inquisitive mind, a lot of guts, and a lot of real moxie into knowing what to touch and what not to touch to stay alive—because you could blow yourself out of there in a heartbeat.[16]

But one did not have to go underground to be in danger of booby traps. Trip wires set up along trails, in underwater places where soldiers must cross, and in seemingly innocuous places in villages could maim or kill without warning. The trauma and stress on battle-weary, shell-shocked soldiers was incalculable.

What We're Really Facing

In addition to the approximately 58,000 U.S. soldiers killed, more than 300,000 Americans were injured in this military conflict with a largely invisible enemy. Our forces inflicted heavy damage as well, with our B-52 bombers being an especially potent weapon. But in retrospect, our ignorance of the enemy's tactics of guerrilla warfare resulted in far more American casualties than would have been the case had we understood his strategy from the beginning.

The same thing is true of spiritual warfare.

A pastor called us just yesterday, traumatized by the news that his teenage daughter, a believer in Christ, was not only depressed and struggling with an eating disorder, but recently had been cutting herself with a razor as well. He had no idea this kind of thing went on, and he and his wife were devastated. He wondered if this self-destructive behavior could be demonically provoked.

Last week a very distraught mother called us. Her young son's teacher and a social worker had told her the boy was schizophrenic because he has been hearing voices in his head. She is convinced that what they believe to be a mental illness, in this case is actually a spiritual attack.

Also this past week, a discipler of young women called us, hoping to find answers in Christ to help a 20-year-old suffering from almost nightly full-blown panic attacks.

Recently a former marine sergeant was brought to his knees when he discovered that a trusted family friend had sexually abused two of his young sons while they were sleeping over at his house. One of the boys, aged five, was already exhibiting erotic behavior with other people. He called us, desperate to know how to help his sons find freedom and healing.

Four couples at a recent marriage conference confessed that their attendance at the event was their last hope for a marriage torn apart by adultery.

Pornography and other sexual addictions. Violence. Sexual abuse. Drug addiction. Alcoholism. Eating disorders. Dark, depressive moods. Guilt. Shame. Fear. Anxiety. Anger out of control. Bitterness. Harassing or blasphemous thoughts. Thoughts of suicide. The litany of suffering and torment from people's own sin and their victimization by others' sin goes on and on.

The question often asked is, "Are these problems spiritual, psychological, or physiological?" The answer is that they are often all of the above.

Our problems always involve the spiritual area of our lives because every struggle affects our relationship with God. Plus, the possibility of being tempted, accused, deceived, threatened, and even physically attacked by the powers of darkness is an ever-present reality. (It is certainly never safe to take off the armor of God.)

In addition, our problems are always psychological, for they affect our mind (what we believe), our emotions (how we feel), and our will (the decisions we make).

Finally, spiritual and psychological problems can result in physical health issues and vice versa.

The complexity of human bondage is at times maddening, and the resolution of such entrapment can seem next to impossible. We can feel as confused and frustrated as those soldiers who were trying to engage an enemy they couldn't see. Though a complete analysis of all the whys of sin and suffering is well beyond the scope of this book, in the rest of this chapter we want to shine more light into the dark tunnel network of our spiritual enemies.

Throwing Light on the Enemies

The Bible teaches that we are up against three primary enemies: the world, the flesh, and the devil.

The *world* (Greek, *kosmos*) refers to the cultural philosophies, practices, and paraphernalia of people who are opposed to God. The apostle John warns us,

> *Do not love the world nor the things in the world. If anyone loves the world, the love of the Father is not in him. For all that is in the world, the lust of the flesh and the lust of the eyes and the boastful pride of life, is not from the Father, but is from the world. The world is passing away, and also its lusts; but the one who does the will of God lives forever* (1 John 2:15-17).

Things in this world appeal to the lust of the flesh (our human appetites out of control), the lust of the eyes (our consuming desire to possess what is beautiful), and the boastful pride of life (the selfish passion to appear successful, smart, powerful, wealthy, religious, and so on). None of these things are part of God's good provision for us.

The *flesh* is that part of us which was well-trained early in life to operate in self-sufficiency rather than God-dependency. It carries over into adulthood and acts in opposition to God's Spirit, as the apostle Paul described in Galatians 5:16-17:

> Walk by the Spirit, and you will not carry out the desire of the flesh. For the flesh sets its desire against the Spirit, and the Spirit against the flesh; for these are in opposition to one another, so that you may not do the things that you please.

When we speak of a believer in Christ's "flesh," we are not speaking of the physical body itself, but rather the lusts of self-centered living that operate in and through that physical body. Christians have one nature, a new nature of righteousness, being new creations in Christ (2 Corinthians 5:17). There is, however, stll a lingering element within the believer that is trained to respond to sin. This self-sufficient "flesh" is not a second nature but a pesky propensity to do evil that will remain until we go home to be with Christ.

Fleshly deeds include the sexual sins of mind and body, the spiritual sins of worshiping false gods, witchcraft, drug and alcohol addictions, wild parties, strife and quarrels, jealousy and envy, angry outbursts, and other things like these (see Galatians 5:22-23).

The *devil* controls the world system (1 John 5:19) and tries to entice us to love the things of the world rather than Christ. One of his names is "tempter" (see, for example, Matthew 4:3). He will aggressively use the things we see, hear, taste, touch, and smell in order to seek to lure us into sin. In addition, sometimes "out of the blue" he will plant a tempting thought in our minds (for example, a critical judgment of a person's motives) to see if we'll take the bait and go down his road. The bottom line is that Satan and his demons are exploiters of the flaws in our character, weaknesses in our will, and chinks in our spiritual armor. The devil is especially ruthless in his attack when he detects that we are seeking to get our needs for acceptance, security, and significance met outside of who we are in Christ..

However, the flesh can also be the source of temptation in these areas without the devil's help. The flesh tries to get us to milk attention, pleasure, and approval from the world around us rather than seeking God and His provision. James wrote,

> Let no one say when he is tempted, "I am being tempted by God"; for God cannot be tempted by evil, and He Himself does not tempt anyone. But each one is tempted when he is carried away and enticed by his own lust. Then when lust has conceived, it gives birth to sin; and when sin is accomplished, it brings forth death. Do not be deceived, my beloved brethren (James 1:13-16).

So how might these three enemies attempt to triple-team us and trap us in the spiritual "crime" of sin? Using legal language, the flesh provides the *means* (using our physical body); the devil, acting as tempter and deceiver, provides the *motive* (by lying to us and making us think sin is a good thing); and the world provides the *opportunity* (through the people, places, and things around us that are in opposition to God and His will). Neil Anderson and Tim Warner help us understand this three-pronged assault:

> Discussions of spiritual warfare sooner or later get around to asking what the relationship is between the world, the flesh, and the devil. Paul introduces all three elements into his definitive statement about this warfare in Ephesians 2:1-3. Notice the way he links the world, the flesh, and the devil together. He does not suggest that sometimes it is the world we are dealing with, sometimes the flesh, and sometimes the devil. Paul sees them working so closely together that you really can't understand one without seeing the way it relates to the others.[17]

The authors conclude their analysis of the passage by saying,

So, in talking about the world, the flesh, and the devil, we need to understand that it is not all one or all the other. Most of the time it is not even mostly one or the other. They work together, and we need a strategy for resistance that takes into account all three without allowing an emphasis on one of them to dominate.[18]

One of the Dirtiest Tricks

Since a plague of pornography and sexual addiction has swept into the church, we will use that issue as a prime example. However, the principles of warfare and the battle plan for freedom that we will begin to unveil at the end of this chapter (and continue in the next) go far beyond the problem of pornography. The truths we will lay out have helped many saints suffering from all the areas of bondage mentioned in this chapter (and more) to find freedom in Christ.

The sick industry we call pornography is now a $10-billion-a-year business in America, ranking it up there with the money spent annually on professional sports, music, or movies. In 2002, the U.S. pornography industry churned out 11,000 new adult videotape and DVD releases, with well over 800 million rentals that year.[19]

One of the most serious infections of pornography among Christians is with church leadership. Sadly, one out of every seven calls received on the Focus on the Family Pastoral Care Line is in reference to Internet pornography.[20] According to Steve Arterburn, co-director of New Life Clinics, the roots of sexual addiction in a church leader can be a thirsty soul looking for love in all the wrong places:

> One of the common threads that we find in people who end up in a sexual addiction is that in their early childhood there were many problems, especially in the area of tremendously high expectations from their parents but very little affirmation when they did achieve whatever they wanted to achieve.

So, good enough was never enough. They were always looking for 25 percent more to satisfy them or to satisfy their parents. Now that they're in ministry, they may have a very satisfying ministry, but in their emptiness and in their despair, they're not able to enjoy their ministry. They are looking for something else, and this hungry soul eventually succumbs to the temptations. Once you've tasted this forbidden sex, of course, it is very, very addictive. That's how they get trapped.[21]

In the case of pornography, let's create a scenario to see how a trap might be sprung. A man has been working long hours, late nights. He comes home and finds his wife, who is also the busy mother of three young children, exhausted and already in bed asleep. The man decides to check e-mails to unwind, and as he goes online he has a fleeting thought to take a quick peek at a pornographic Web site. Though such a temptation could come from the devil, in this case, let's say this thought comes from his *flesh,* which picks up on his body's need for sexual release and responds with self-pity and anger at feeling cheated by his boss (who overworks him) and his wife (who is asleep). The erotic thought creates a state of physical arousal, and so the man can't wait to check out the Web site. By this time he has already mentally justified his actions.

The *world* gladly obliges his fleshly lust with countless Web sites that he can choose from depending on how "soft"- or "hard"-core he wants his porn. He picks one he overheard a guy at work drooling over, finds the sights and sounds to his liking, and experiences sexual gratification.

After the thrill is over, his passion dies down, and he has a chance to consider what he has done. Then the third member of this evil trio attacks. The *devil,* or more likely one of his demonic henchmen, moves in for the kill. The strategy he chooses this time is called "accusation." Accusation is the verbal or mental harassment designed to convince us that we are less than who God says we are in Christ. Thoughts, and consequent feelings, of guilt, shame, worthlessness, helplessness, and condemnation are typical.

In this man's case the accusations overwhelm him with an artillery barrage of disparaging thoughts in his mind. These thoughts may be trying to mimic the voice of God or his own guilty conscience, but they could very well sound something like this:

"I can't believe you did that! What a hypocrite you are, *Christian!* Your wife will find out. She is going to be devastated. She'll never trust you again. And she shouldn't. You have crossed over the line. You're going to become an addict. You'll do it again tomorrow night—you know you will. No matter how repentant you're feeling right now, you liked it and you're hooked." And that's just the beginning of the torment that's unleashed against him.

The man has been ambushed by a guerrilla attack involving an invisible enemy who mercilessly assaults his mind until he is wallowing in guilt, shame, fear, and regret. And unless he gets help and gets it fast, he *could* well become hooked.

The devil lurks and works in the darkness of shame, seclusion, and denial, seeking to lure us deeper and deeper into bondage; God is light and operates in the brightness of truth, honesty, and genuine transparency, seeking to release us into freedom. Sadly, for many men, the secret world of pornography, and sexual gratification without the responsibility of commitment and the hard work that true relationships require, becomes a fatal attraction.

This epidemic of sexual addiction is not limited to men, however. For women, the lure may be more in a yearning for romance, tenderness, and emotional intimacy, but it can lead to the same devastating consequences. Dr. Harry Schaumberg, veteran counselor of those struggling with sexual addictions, warns in his book *False Intimacy* that

> statistics don't begin to capture the countless, agonizing stories
> of the victims of sexual addiction in the church: wives betrayed

by their husbands, husbands betrayed by their wives, congregations paralyzed by scandal, careers ruined, marriages and families destroyed, and the image of Christians smeared.[22]

Are the Resources We've Been Given Sufficient?

The questions that cry out for answers are, Is this battle for the mind a winnable war? Is it truly possible for those caught in sin's snares and by the devil's dirtiest tricks to escape into the freedom Christ purchased at Calvary? Can temptation be overcome? Can addictions be broken? Can the voice of the accuser be silenced? Can deceit and denial be exposed and truth embraced from the heart?

What we are really asking is, "Is Jesus Christ, along with the resources He has given us in the Word of God, the body of Christ, and the Holy Spirit, sufficient to defeat the enemy?"

The answer to every one of these questions is a resounding *yes!* But where do you begin? You can find our answer on where to start in the following warfare strategies. These are written primarily for believers who want to help others in bondage. If *you* are one of those trapped individuals, then apply these to yourself while wasting no time in getting help.

The first attack against bondage is always *prayer.* Pray that the person in bondage would get out of denial and see the predicament they're in. Pray that they would realize that apart from Christ they can do nothing to extricate themselves (John 15:5). Pray that they would see that God is forgiving, good, and all-powerful, and that they would understand that He knows the path to their freedom. Pray that the lies the enemy has been feeding the person would be exposed for what they are and that the person would yearn for freedom and come to hate their sin. Pray that hope would be restored (Romans 15:13).

Even though we devoted a whole chapter earlier in this book to the importance of prayer, we feel that it's critical to say more. We simply cannot overstate its importance. Prayer opens doors that no man or power of hell can shut.

As you pray, recognize that sometimes things get worse before they get better. In order for some people to look up, they've got to hit rock bottom. As long as they can come up with one more technique of self-rescue, most people caught in addictions will try to pull themselves up by their own bootstraps.

Though this may be painful, ask the Lord to bring the person to the point of brokenness (the state of utter despair and realization of the inability of self-repair). Psalm 51:17 puts it this way: "The sacrifices of God are a broken spirit; a broken and a contrite heart, O God, You will not despise." (Because the spiritual battle for a soul caught in bondage can be quite intense, sometimes the Lord calls His saints to *fast* as they pray. We encourage you to pick up a book such as *Fasting for Spiritual Breakthrough* by Elmer Towns or *God's Chosen Fast* by Arthur Wallis to study up on this subject. Fasting is a weapon too often neglected.)

The second assault against bondage must be *unconditional love and acceptance.* By showing these, you are not condoning any sinful behavior. Rather, you are accepting the person as someone with inherent dignity—created in the image of God and (if a Christian) in union with Christ. Remember that love "bears all things, believes all things, hopes all things, endures all things. Love never fails" (1 Corinthians 13:7-8). Perhaps the most potent aspect of God's love is that it never, ever gives up. Ask God to show you what His love looks like for the person trapped in sin.

True freedom from sin's control and true healing from sin's wounds must always come in the context of relationships with other Christians. Isolation is one of the devil's most effective weapons, and that's why the Bible continually reminds us of our responsibility toward one another. "Love one another" (1 John 4:7), "encourage one another" (Hebrews 3:13), and "teach and admonish one another" (Colossians 3:16 NIV) are just a sampling of the scriptural exhortations to live out our Christian lives in community.

The devil wants to use guilt, shame, and the fear of being judged and condemned by the church to keep people trapped in their secret world of sin. Don't let him score a point here. All the talk in the world about the love of God—without the assurance of real flesh-and-blood believers living out that love—is worthless. "Little children, let us not love with word or with tongue, but in deed and truth" (1 John 3:18). "Beloved, if God so loved us, we also ought to love one another. No one has seen God at any time; if we love one another, God abides in us, and His love is perfected in us" (1 John 4:11-12). And of course, this kind of love is only possible through the power of the Holy Spirit.

Third, *truth*, when brought in behind the "air cover" of prayer and the "artillery fire" of love, can truly be a "rescue helicopter" for a person held hostage by the powers of darkness. In the next chapter we'll talk about how to bring in truth that's surrounded by grace as the means to set captives free. For now, it is enough to know that Jesus taught us,

> *If you continue in My word, then you are truly disciples of Mine; and you will know the truth, and the truth will make you free... Truly, truly, I say to you, everyone who commits sin is the slave of sin. The slave does not remain in the house forever; the son does remain forever. So if the Son makes you free, you will be free indeed* (John 8:31-32,34-36).

Every sin that controls us is fueled by lies that we have believed. *Every* sin. There are no exceptions. And once you recognize the lie, reject it as such, and embrace the truth, then freedom comes. What I have just described is called *repentance*—a change of mind that results in a change of life.

When repentance comes—true repentance—then all heaven breaks loose!

> *Dear heavenly Father, all this talk about my enemies is a little unnerving. But I thank You that nowhere in Your Word do you instruct me to be afraid of the devil. "Greater is He who is in*

[me] than he who is in the world." That's what 1 John 4:4 says, and I choose to believe it. I refuse to be anxious, but instead I will "be of sober spirit" and "on the alert." I admit to You, Jesus, that I am not strong enough in myself to resist temptation, silence accusation, or sniff out deception. I need You to be my spiritual radar to grant me that kind of discernment. And in the areas where I continue to fall and fail, I cry out to You to rescue me, dear Lord. I thank You that nothing is too difficult for You, and I stand against the enemy's attempt to steal hope from me. I trust that freedom is for me, too, even as I continue to take responsibility for choosing truth and getting the help I need. In the name of Jesus, who is the way, truth, and life, I pray, amen.

For further Scripture study on the Lord's intervention on behalf of those in bondage:

Take unhurried time and pray through and meditate on Psalm 107.

Questions for reflection and discussion:

There were a variety of areas of bondage mentioned in this chapter. Have you struggled with any of them? If so, ask the Lord what lies you have been believing that have fueled that struggle. If not, spend some time thanking the Lord for His gracious protection.

In what ways are you being tempted? Why do you feel you are particularly vulnerable to this particular temptation or these particular temptations? Ask the Lord to reveal this to you, keeping in mind that exposure to a particular sin at any early age can sometimes predispose us to that sin.

Are there any accusations that you have believed about yourself that are contrary to the truths about who you are in Christ? (You may want to review some of these truths in chapter 2.) Ask the Lord to strengthen you to believe and walk in accordance with the truth—despite what your feelings, family, friends, or foes might tell you.

Do you feel like the enemy has managed to dig a complex system of spiritual tunnels under you or your home, or perhaps even your church? For further study on understanding, exposing, and defeating the powers of darkness, we encourage you to read the following books by Dr. Neil Anderson:

- *Victory over the Darkness*
- *The Bondage Breaker*
- *The Christ-Centered Marriage* (co-authored by Dr. Charles Mylander)
- *Setting Your Church Free* (co-authored by Dr. Charles Mylander)

7
POWs

In 1970 I was part of a very large military force that President Nixon ordered to invade Cambodia. A 25-mile limit was set on how far we could go into this "neutral" country in order to take out enemy depots and disrupt supplies and troop shipments streaming down the Ho Chi Minh trail into South Vietnam. Our unit set up in a makeshift staging area just north of Tay Ninh City, at a place known as the "elephant's ear" because of the shape of the Vietnam–Cambodia border.

Our helicopter unit flew a number of different missions during this invasion, and for the first three days and nights I don't remember sleeping much, if at all. We were in the air most of the time, the action was so intense. Even though the enemy had advance warning of our invasion, many troops refused to retreat behind the 25-mile line of demarcation and chose to stay and fight to the death.

One of our missions was to do bomb damage assessments after U.S. Air Force jets had made their raids into the area. The North Vietnamese had a number of SAM (surface-to-air missile) sites set up to take out our jets. While conducting our missions we would often see a number of our pilots ejecting from their jet aircraft after being hit.

We would always do our best to rescue them before they were captured. Too often we couldn't get to them fast enough, and they would be caught by the NVA and taken to prisoner-of-war camps in North Vietnam.

One cloudy, rainy day in March 1970, I was flying over a place called the Straight Edge Woods. It was a large, thick, ominous stand of triple-canopy forest straddling the Cambodian–Vietnamese border between Cu Chi and Tay Ninh. Normally I would have avoided this place like the plague. It was a dangerous stronghold of the enemy, and we had no "friendlies" near enough to help us if we were to get in trouble there. A few weeks earlier a rocket-propelled grenade had exploded just behind my tail rotor, and so I hated—and feared—this place with a passion.

As I headed south along the edge of the woods just east of the huge, muddy Van Co Dong River, one of our ground units that was operating near the area spotted us in the air and contacted us by radio. They thought they had just spotted a patrol of NVA regulars marching several captured GIs north through the woods toward the Cambodian border. They were headed to a POW camp.

The message sent chills through my entire crew as they listened over their headsets. Every one of us knew what happened to captured American soldiers. For them, survival during the march was doubtful, and death would be welcomed should they make it all the way to the prison camp. There was no way we were going to let this happen to them if we could help it.

I radioed my command center at Cu Chi and told my commanding officer where we were and about our change of flight plans. I did not wait for a response or permission. Immediately I turned my aircraft toward this jungle hell. We quickly dropped to treetop level, 200 feet above the forest floor, and started searching through the dense foliage for trails and any sign of our friends.

This maneuver put us all in great danger of enemy fire, but my entire crew was ready to jump out of the helicopter if needed in order to free our fellow soldiers from captivity.

We searched as long as our fuel load would allow, following the trails we could catch sight of through the canopy. We spotted what we thought were a few makeshift camps or possible holding stations.

We even landed in a few of these spots in the hope of rescuing our men, though we had no gunship backup.

Over and over again, signs of their presence were there, but they were nowhere in sight. With little fuel left to continue, we were forced to abandon our search. Turning that helicopter around to return to base camp was one of the most disheartening moments in my tour of duty in Nam.

When captured, many of our POWs were sent to the Hoa Lo prison complex in the center of Hanoi, North Vietnam. Our soldiers nick-named this place "Heartbreak Hotel" and the "Hanoi Hilton." "New Guy Village" was where new POWs were received, and "Las Vegas" was where torture sessions were regularly held.

These compounds were small and dirty. Your legs were forced into shackles with a pipe and rope to lock them in place. Your arms were tied behind your back from above the elbow to the wrists. A foot from a guard placed in your back would tighten the ropes so that they cut into your bones. You wouldn't bleed because these bindings would act like a tourniquet.

You were thrown into a space not much bigger than your body, where you lay on a cement slab. No medical care was given, and two meals a day of pumpkin or cabbage soup would keep you alive but without the nutrients to ward off disease. Sitting in your own waste with no ability to ward off the rats and spiders crawling over you was terrifying. And with no windows, the darkness was complete.

No one can be taught to survive such brutality. The cruelty was designed to break your resistance and provide the enemy with sadistic pleasure as he exerted his power over you. In this kind of bondage, you can only maintain your sanity and hold on for so long.

Every soldier dreaded the possibility of becoming a prisoner of war. Medals of Honor were awarded to men who did everything in their power to save their fellow soldiers' lives and prevent them from being taken captive. Most of these awards were bestowed posthumously...

because someone was willing to lay down his life for a friend. Jesus said there is no greater love than this (John 15:13).

None of us set out to be heroes. We were all just scared young boys, called to be soldiers to do a job for our country. Some of us might have been more committed, resourceful, stubborn, or naïve than other soldiers. But every one of us was ready to face what was in the darkness because we were fighting for one another. Whether we lived or died, we would do it for each other—because that was all most of us had.

—

During those days in Vietnam, a seed was planted in my heart that did not begin to grow or bear fruit until after I came to know Jesus Christ as my Savior and Lord. This was the unquenchable yearning to rescue those who are trapped by the enemy. I have since come to understand that perhaps 85 percent or more of the body of Christ is in varying degrees oppressed and in bondage to the world, the flesh, and the devil. These believers are spiritual prisoners of war. And by God's enabling grace, they must be set free.

After coming to Christ and spending three years of intense discipleship training and growth at our local church in Wisconsin, Kathy and I sensed the Lord calling us into full-time Christian service. We applied with the Evangelical Free Church Mission and were assigned to Zaire (now Congo), Africa, in 1983 as career missionaries.

Late in 1984 I was attending a pastors' conference in a small rural village in Zaire. I was walking with a group of pastors when we noticed a teenage boy following us. He made his way to the front of our group and stared directly into my eyes. I could tell there was something seriously wrong with him, and his intent toward us appeared to be malevolent. Our group stopped and I asked him in the trade language of Lingala, *"Ozali nani?"* This, literally translated, is "Who are you?" but is generally understood as "What is your name?" His response was,

"Tozali mingi"—"We are many." It was clear that this was the same type of evil presence I had experienced in my past, but I still had no idea how to respond to it, let alone how to help this young man be set free.

I expected the native pastors to know what to do. After all, this was their land and people. But they seemed as confused and fearful as I was. After 60 years of missionary presence in Zaire, they had been deeply infected with our Western worldview.

Rescuing Captives—Through a Power Encounter?

How does this affect Christians in their conduct of spiritual warfare? Dr. Timothy Warner, veteran missionary and missiologist comments:

> Unfortunately, not many missionaries or evangelists or pastors enter into their ministries prepared to handle demonic problems. On the mission field, it is often assumed that national pastors will be able to take care of such situations, but that is not always true, especially if they have been educated in Western missionary-run schools. It is true, however, that the demonstration of power in such confrontations may be a key to unlocking an apparently resistant people group.[23]

Upon returning to the United States in 1986, I attended a course offered by Trinity Evangelical Divinity School entitled "Power Encounter," which was taught by Dr. Warner. It was here that I came to realize just how much my Western worldview had prevented me from understanding the spiritual realm and its influence on the life of both believers and nonbelievers.

Upon completion of this course, my wife and I were invited by Dr. Warner to be his prayer partners in a personal counseling session, looking to apply what we had learned in the classroom. Knowing that we would be helping a Christian evangelical seminary student, we were confident nothing weird would happen. And that was fine with us!

On an evening soon after that, we sat down with a young single man. After we started the session with prayer, he began to share his story. He recounted a 300-year history of witchcraft in his family background. He then shared how he had entered into a personal relationship with Jesus Christ through a campus ministry during college. While there he felt called by God to enter full-time Christian service, and that was why he was attending seminary. But he was having serious problems.

One key element in his history, he indicated, was that a demonic curse had been placed on all firstborn males in the family line so that all of them would die before entering marriage. As he spoke he was having trouble controlling his vocal cords and could not stop clearing his throat. Kathy and I had no idea what we were about to experience.

Dr. Warner prayed and commanded all demonic spirits present to manifest themselves. His purpose was to determine if any were present and whether they were the source of the man's difficulty in speaking.

No sooner was the prayer finished than several different, distinct, and evil voices began speaking through this student. The voices claimed that they had the right to be in his body and that we were powerless to help. With the kind of foul language they used, I now had a profound sense of why Scripture refers to them as "unclean spirits" (see Matthew 10:1; Mark 1:23,26; Revelation 18:2).

As the session went on, different demonic personalities would take control of the young man's vocal cords. They cursed us and continued to refuse to leave even though commanded to do so in the name of the Lord Jesus Christ. I could see in the man's eyes that he felt helpless to do anything and that he desperately wanted us to help him be free.

The session went on for hours. Sometimes the demons would answer our questions about their names and why they were harassing this believer, but they steadfastly refused to leave. In the end, we finished the session exhausted, frustrated, and defeated, feeling as miserable as I had when I hadn't been able to find and rescue my fellow soldiers who were captured in Nam.

What I just described would typically be called "deliverance ministry," or a "power-encounter" approach to liberating a believer from past or present demonic control. For many years Christian leaders had been recognizing that Christians were still wrestling with demonic forces in their lives after their conversion, but they had no other method than this by which to help these saints resolve their spiritual conflicts.

Rescuing Captives—Through the *Truth*

Then, in 1988, southern California's Fuller Seminary hosted a symposium of 40 scholars who were teaching at the graduate level about spiritual warfare. One of these scholars was Dr. Neil Anderson, who at the time taught at Talbot School of Theology. At this gathering, Dr. Anderson shared his departure from the "power-encounter"[24] approach and his journey into a different way of dealing with the demonic:

> My first approach was to get a demon to expose itself and then command it to come out. Usually this resulted in a great deal of trauma for the person, and one would have to wonder who was more powerful. Although progress was made, the episode would often have to be repeated again. This is where the Epistles [New Testament letters to churches and individuals] come in. It is the believer's responsibility to resist, renounce, forgive and confess. It is not what the counselor does that results in freedom, it is what the counselee believes, confesses and renounces. The counselor acts as a facilitator. I have not attempted to "cast out a demon" in several years, but I have seen hundreds find freedom in Christ.[25]

Contrary to the prevailing strategy, Dr. Anderson had come to the conclusion that it is not *power* that sets the captive free, but *truth*. This agrees with Jesus' prayer for His disciples in John 17:15-17:

> *I do not ask You to take them out of the world, but to keep them from the evil one. They are not of the world, even as I am not of the world. Sanctify them in the truth; Your word is truth.*

After graduation from seminary in 1988, Kathy and I transitioned from our missionary work in Africa to a church-planting ministry in Miami, Florida. Most of our new converts there had been involved in Santería, a mixture of Old World Catholicism and African spiritism. Though we were learning, we still did not have a good understanding of how to help these new converts resolve their personal and spiritual conflicts.

In 1991 our church-planting team invited Dr. Tim Warner to Miami to conduct a spiritual-warfare conference. It was here that we were first introduced to the concepts found in Dr. Anderson's landmark books *Victory over the Darkness* and *The Bondage Breaker*.

Dr. Warner had participated in the 1988 Symposium at Fuller Seminary. By that time he had already been profoundly impacted by Dr. Anderson's books and teachings and was in full agreement with what he presented there. He shared with us what he had been learning. Because of what Dr. Warner taught us, for the first time I realized why I was having such a difficult time trying to disciple our new converts and get them meaningfully involved in our church. Why was it? Because the majority of these people, though born again, were still identifying themselves as victims of their past rather than as victorious products of the cross of Jesus Christ. My attempts at discipling them were lacking the essential ingredient of grounding them in their identity in Christ, and therefore they were not growing.

What I needed to be doing was *discipleship counseling*. Dr. Anderson describes more of his journey into understanding this process:

As a pastor, I believed that Christ was the answer and truth would set people free, but I really didn't know how. People at my church had problems for which I didn't have answers, but God did. When the Lord called me to teach at Talbot School of Theology, I was searching for answers myself. Slowly I began to understand how to help people resolve their personal and spiritual conflicts through genuine repentance by submitting to God and resisting the devil. My seminary education had taught me about the kingdom of God, but not about the kingdom of darkness...

Through countless hours of intense counseling with defeated Christians, I began to understand the battle for their minds and how they could be transformed by the renewing of their minds. I am saddened by how we have separated the ministries of discipleship and counseling in our churches. Christian discipleship too often has become an impersonal program, although good theological material is being used. Christian counseling has been intensely personal, but often lacks good theology. I believe discipleship and counseling are biblically the same. If you were a good discipler you would be a good counselor and vice versa. Discipleship counseling is the process where two or more people meet together in the presence of Christ, learn how the truth of God's Word can set them free and thus are able to conform to the image of God as they walk by faith in the power of the Holy Spirit.[26]

A Process for Encountering the Truth

This method of dealing with the demonic that was birthed through Dr. Anderson and Freedom in Christ Ministries has now been adopted by thousands of church leaders, disciplers, pastors, and counselors worldwide. We like to view it as a *truth-authority encounter.* It is a time when the Lord Jesus Christ, the Truth Himself, exercises His authority over sin and Satan through the person being counseled, as he or she submits to God in repentance and obedient faith. Although the encounter often involves a facilitator (or "encourager," as we call him or her) and a prayer partner, many individuals have taken themselves through this process—which we call "The Steps to Freedom in Christ."[27]

The Steps to Freedom in Christ focus on seven major areas in which believers in Christ can fall prey to deception and bondage. Here are those areas of emphasis:

- *Counterfeit vs. Real*
  The individual confesses and renounces all past or present involvement with cults, the occult, and non-Christian religions and practices.

- *Deception vs. Truth*
  The individual confesses and repents of ways in which he or she has bought into the lies of the world system, and ways in which he or she has been self-deceived or has wrongly defended himself.

- *Bitterness vs. Forgiveness*
  The person makes the choice to forgive from the heart all the people who have hurt, abused, neglected, or offended him or her. This step also involves accepting God's forgiveness of oneself in Christ, as well as the releasing of any anger toward and lies believed about God Himself.

- *Rebellion vs. Submission*
  All acts and attitudes of rebellion toward human authorities and God Himself are confessed and a submissive servant-heart is chosen.

- *Pride vs. Humility*
  The individual confesses and repents of numerous ways in which a self-sufficient, haughty, or proud spirit has manifested itself.

- *Bondage vs. Freedom*
  In this step, fleshly sins (with special emphases on sexual sins, controlling fears, and other areas) are confessed and repented of and the choice to walk by faith is made.

- *Curses vs. Blessings*
  The person renounces all generational sins in his or her life and declares his or her new identity in Christ rather than being "in Adam," then commits to a walk of faith in and submission to God in the power of the Holy Spirit.

By prayerful dependence upon the Holy Spirit and repentance from all sin that He reveals, the individual going through the Steps follows the biblical pattern of James 4:7: "Submit therefore to God. Resist the devil and he will flee from you." In essence, what the believer is doing is conforming to the writer of Hebrews' exhortation:

> *Let us also lay aside every encumbrance and the sin which so easily entangles us, and let us run with endurance the race that is set before us, fixing our eyes on Jesus* (Hebrews 12:1-2).

A believer in Christ simply cannot run the race toward Christian maturity until he or she is free. The Steps to Freedom in Christ are an effective tool in helping God's people be released from the control of the world, flesh, and devil,[28] and we heartily encourage you to go through them if you have never done so or have not done so recently.

Helping Others Encounter the Truth

What we must keep in mind when helping others go through a process like the Steps is that the only Wonderful Counselor is the Lord Jesus Himself (Isaiah 9:6) and He is the One who came to set captives free (Luke 4:18). The Steps to Freedom in Christ have never set anyone free, and they never will. They are, however, an excellent tool that God has graciously chosen to use. But like any tool, the Steps are only as useful as the skill of the one using them. Therefore we do well to follow the apostle Paul's instruction in 2 Timothy 2:24-26 when seeking to set captives free in Christ.

> *The Lord's bond-servant must not be quarrelsome, but be kind to all, able to teach, patient when wronged, with gentleness correcting those who are in opposition, if perhaps God may grant them repentance leading to the knowledge of the truth, and they may come to their senses and escape from the snare of the devil, having been held captive by him to do his will.*

Based on this scripture, here are some key points to keep in mind:

- We must be walking in obedient surrender to the Lord and be filled with the Holy Spirit in order to truly help others.

- We must persuasively instruct others with kindness and gentleness, but not try to argue people into submission to our will or opinion. Those we counsel must submit willingly to God or our efforts are futile.

- We must not react defensively if people we are counseling get angry or attack us verbally. Man's anger never achieves God's righteousness (James 1:19-20).

- We must remember that repentance is a gift from God and so it is His responsibility to bring the one we're counseling to the place of repenting from the heart.

- In order for someone to be set free from the devil's control, repentance that leads to the knowledge of the truth must occur.

Both Rich and I have had the privilege of seeing thousands of God's people set free through the use of the Steps to Freedom in Christ. Aside from seeing someone radically saved from sin, there is nothing more rewarding than seeing a captive saint released from spiritual bondage. By God's grace, He will use you, too, to rescue spiritual POWs.

The question that is burning in our hearts right now is this, however: Are *you* walking in the freedom that is yours in Christ? If you know today that you have issues in your life that are hindering you from the fullness of the Spirit, don't wait. Get help today. You can begin by praying along with us:

> *Dear heavenly Father, I thank You that Jesus was bound to the cross so I could be free. He was scourged so I could be healed. He died so I could have life. I ask You, Lord, to search me and know my heart. Test me and know my anxious thoughts, and see if there is any hurtful way in me. And please lead me in Your everlasting way. Open my eyes to any ways in which I have surrendered ground to the devil in my life so I can close those doors and present those areas back to You. Where I need repentance, please grant it to me. Enable me to come to my senses and escape from the enemy's snares. I no longer want to live in captivity to his will, but I want to say, "Not my will, but Yours be done, O God." Please unleash all Your power, grace, truth, and authority in my life so I can experience the freedom Christ purchased for me at Calvary. In the name of the Crucified, Risen, Ascended, and Glorified Lord Jesus Christ I pray, amen.*

For further Scripture study
on setting captives free:

Prayerfully read through Isaiah 58 and 61.

Questions for reflection or discussion:

Why is a clear understanding of biblical truth so important in our efforts to walk in freedom? (See John 8:44 and Romans 12:1-2.)

As you read through the brief summary of the seven Steps to Freedom in Christ, were there any ones in particular that you recognized were areas in which you need freedom? If so, what were they?

Do you agree that a truth-authority encounter approach to setting captives free will, in the long run, be more effective than a "power encounter," or deliverance approach? Why or why not?

As you try to help other people, what character qualities and skills in serving that are mentioned in 2 Timothy 2:24-26 do you need to ask God to be especially developing in your life?

8
Friendly Fire

There were many occasions during my tour in Vietnam when we brought overwhelming firepower to bear so quickly and in such close proximity to our own soldiers in combat that there was a very real danger of injuring or killing them. This could be the case at any time, but engagements after dark required extra caution on the part of those delivering ordnance near our troops.

It was the hour after midnight. We were flying another Nighthawk mission over numerous ambush patrols scattered across the rice paddies and jungles. There was no moon that night, making it difficult to figure out exactly where we were as well as the lay of the land below us. To make matters worse, there were no lighted cities or highways by which we could get our bearings; it was pitch black on the ground. Pinpointing targets without shooting our own people presented a formidable challenge that night.

We received a radio call from one of the ground units. Their message came whispered so they wouldn't be heard by the enemy soldiers approaching their position. This six-man patrol was hunkered down in foxholes near a supply trail…as VC soldiers too numerous to engage moved past them.

The enemy was so close to their position they could see and hear them. Normally one of our men would have put a strobe light on his helmet to help me locate their exact position, but this time it was not possible. Nevertheless, they were requesting our gunship support to fire on this trail just a few feet in front of them. I had a general idea of their location simply by the grid coordinates on my map, but it was very risky.

One of our tactics as pilots was to fly some distance away from these ambush patrols, then drop down to an altitude just above treetop level. The VC knew we were flying above them from the sound of our rotor blades, but they couldn't see us because we never flew with our lights on. When we were out of earshot, they would think we had flown to another location and were no longer a threat. In reality, we would turn back toward them and drop to the nap of the earth so our helicopter could not be heard until we were right on top of them.

As I drove the aircraft at maximum speed as close to the tops of the trees as I dared, I could see what appeared to be our unit's location. I ordered everyone to lock and load their weapons. Over the intercom I told my gunner to open fire with our minigun, which was mounted out the left side of the cargo bay, just behind my seat. The firepower of this weapon was devastating, with the capacity to put a bullet into every square foot of an area the size of a football field. Using it ensured that nothing would be left standing in the target area.

As soon as my gunner pulled the trigger—the sound of which was deafening—I heard a scream in my headset from the radio operator on the ground. I will take that terrible sound to my grave. He was shouting at the top of his lungs, "Shut it off! You are shooting your own men!"

Immediately I banked the aircraft hard right and pulled up. This caused my gunner's trajectory to move up along the treeline and tear down some of the jungle foliage. We barely made it over the tops of the trees ourselves. I thought to myself, *What have I done? Have I just killed some of our own men?*

By this time, the enemy knew we were on site, so they scattered into the jungle, dragging with them the bodies of their comrades we had just killed. But I desperately wanted to know if we had just caused some needless casualties of war with our own friendly fire.

When I came back around for a second pass over the LZ, the voice on the radio assured me our soldiers were unharmed, but said our bullets had come within inches of their foxholes. You can't imagine how relieved I felt. Now that it was safer to identify their position and I could see exactly where they were located, I exhausted the remainder of our ammunition around their perimeter and kept watch over them until our fuel supply ran low.

I didn't know the names of the men below us, nor did I ever get to meet them face-to-face. All I knew was their call sign over a radio signal. However, that night, all of us together were gripped by the reality of the danger and potential damage of friendly fire.

Since our conversion to Christ in 1977, Kathy, our two daughters, and I have fought shoulder to shoulder in a spiritual battle we initially understood little about. We entered into this warfare naïvely thinking that Christians, being on the same side, would never do anything to intentionally harm one another. After all, we were fellow soldiers committed to the same vision and mission, weren't we? Why wouldn't we all agree that the most important thing in the world was to glorify God by preaching the gospel, proclaiming release to captives, and setting the oppressed free…together?

The Lord Jesus Himself proclaimed that as His mission statement (see Luke 4:18-19), and the apostle John echoed it, writing that our Lord's purpose in coming was to destroy the devil's works (1 John 3:8). Shouldn't all God's people be on the same page as their Lord?

Unity—God's Design

It is clearly God's design and desire for His children to be unified in obeying the Great Commandment and fulfilling the Great

Commission. Jesus prayed for this in His high priestly prayer, recorded in John 17:14-21:

> *I have given them Your word; and the world has hated them, because they are not of the world, even as I am not of the world. I do not ask You to take them out of the world, but to keep them from the evil one. They are not of the world, even as I am not of the world. Sanctify them in the truth; Your word is truth. As You sent me into the world, I also have sent them into the world. For their sakes I sanctify Myself, that they themselves also may be sanctified in truth.*
>
> *I do not ask on behalf of these alone, but for those also who believe in Me through their word; that they may all be one; even as You, Father, are in Me and I in You, that they also may be in Us, so that the world may believe that You sent Me.*

Two thousand years ago Jesus prayed that we would be unified in love as we lived together behind enemy lines on this fallen planet. Years later, Paul exhorted believers to exhibit the unifying qualities of being of one mind, loving each other, and being united in spirit and intent on one purpose (see Philippians 2:2).

The heart of Jesus has always been that we would show a deep concern and care for one another, demonstrating a unified front so winsome to the unconverted that they would see that Jesus was truly sent from God, His Father. He was not talking about uniformity, but unity in diversity through the sanctifying truth of God's Word. We all have different personality styles, cultural experiences, and theological persuasions. Jesus was not praying that we would all look alike and act alike, only that we would reflect the oneness and unity of His relationship with the Father.

The army did not look like or operate in the same way as the marines. The marines were not identical to the air force. The air force was different from the navy. But we were all on the same side—and fighting side by side for a common cause under a common commander in chief.

Sadly, that has too often not been the case with the body of Christ.

According to current research, each year we are losing about 18,000 pastors and more than 5000 long-term missionaries, many directly or indirectly due to friendly fire. The most common scenario involves interpersonal conflict followed by burnout and moral failure. If Christian leaders are under this kind of pressure, what makes us think those in the ranks are having it any better? If the enemy strikes the shepherds, will not the sheep be scattered?

In the recent book *Less Is More Leadership*, Dale Burke, senior pastor of First Evangelical Free Church in Fullerton, California, comments on the spiritual, moral, and time pressure that church leaders are experiencing today. Of course, this includes the difficulties that stem from contention within their congregations:

> Leadership is tough, and it's getting tougher. And the stress is being felt by leaders at every level. The common assumption is that the solution is to pray harder, work harder, and work longer hours. As a result, leaders today are being stretched until they snap under the pressure of today's fast-paced, high-demand, rapid-change culture. They eventually hit a crisis point at which the health of the leader and organization begin to go downhill.[29]

Back in 1996, World Evangelical Fellowship (WEF) conducted a survey among 553 mission-agency leaders from 14 nations, seeking to uncover the reasons for the abnormal amount of missionary attrition taking place in both the "new and old sending nations." When speaking about the issue, WEF Missions Committee Director, Dr. Bill Taylor, spoke not only of the dangers of "illness, kidnapping and martyrdom" but also mentioned a female missionary who took her own life.[30] Reflecting on his words, the WEF newsletter commented,

> Bill's illustration of the returned missionary in her suicide note expressed how the lack of pastoral attention and understanding

had driven her to take her life…Pastoral intervention is not only needed to avert tragedies, but to help career missionaries be effective in packing heaven with worshippers! The challenge of the unreached peoples can primarily be met through long-term missionaries. We must help the right ones to get there and provide the support they need to stay there.[31]

Giving the Devil an Opportunity

Kathy and I have traveled the world. We have been confronted by *nganga nkisi* (witch doctors) in Central Africa, *curanderos* (psychic healers) in Central America, *santeros* and *santeras* (priests and priestesses of the cult of Santería) in Miami, Florida, and the "juju men" of West Africa. Some of them were intimidating at first, but they all understood the reality of spiritual battle. As we developed a relationship with them and they realized that we were not there to attack them but rather to show them a better way, we found most of them to be pleasant and easy people to talk with.

This has not always been true of our brothers and sisters in Christ. My entire family has been victimized by "friendly fire." It forced us to resign in our early years of ministry, draining away our desire to keep moving forward. Gossip, theological arrogance and inflexibility, contentions over the philosophy of serving, and power struggles for control are all weapons of mass destruction that have damaged us.

Sadly, I must confess that at times I too have been guilty of firing some of these devastating psychological weapons against my own people—out of frustration, pain, or misunderstanding.

Don't get me wrong. I believe with all my heart that there are theological convictions we all should have. These were clearly delineated by the apostle Paul:

> There is one body and one Spirit, just as also you were called in
> one hope of your calling; one Lord, one faith, one baptism, one

God and Father of all who is over all and through all and in all
(Ephesians 4:4-6).

Those are the things to major on, and if we do, the door is wide open for love, which is the perfect bond of unity (Colossians 3:14).

However, we can easily become more committed to our theological and philosophical preferences than we are to loving each other and treating each other with kindness. Overcommitment to our own point of view is an issue of pride that results in much unnecessary conflict. This is sin, and it grieves our God. Paul's heart must have been breaking when he wrote,

> *Be angry, and yet do not sin; do not let the sun go down on your anger, and do not give the devil an opportunity...Let no unwholesome word proceed from your mouth, but only such a word as is good for edification according to the need of the moment, so that it will give grace to those who hear.* Do not grieve the Holy Spirit of God, by whom you were sealed for the day of redemption. *Let all bitterness and wrath and anger and clamor and slander be put away from you, along with all malice. Be kind to one another, tender-hearted, forgiving each other, just as God in Christ also has forgiven you* (Ephesians 4:26-27,29-32).

That scripture ought to wake up every one of us. Unresolved anger in our hearts leaves the door wide open for the devil to operate in our lives! The Greek word for "opportunity" is *topos*, which means a *place*—in this case a base of operations from which the devil can launch a campaign against us. In essence, harboring bitterness and unforgiveness in our hearts will give the enemy opportunity to "undermine—tunnel underneath—our lives." This does not mean that a believer in Christ can be possessed by the devil. We belong to Christ alone and have been purchased by His shed blood (see 1 Peter 1:18-19). However, Satan can wreak havoc on any child of God who refuses to forgive, afflicting his mind, emotions, will, and even body.

How dangerous to angrily hunker down in our denominational, philosophical, methodological, or preferential bunkers and fire salvos at one another in the name of "being right"! Yet that is what too often happens, and by so doing we foolishly leave out a welcome mat for the devil.

Tragically, our track record of getting along as Christians has been abysmal. Hence the need for Paul to implore us

> to walk in a manner worthy of the calling with which you have been called, with all humility and gentleness, with patience, showing tolerance to one another in love, being diligent to preserve the unity of the Spirit in the bond of peace (Ephesians 4:1-3).

Have you ever wondered why, in the middle of the passage on spiritual warfare in Ephesians 6, Paul felt led to remind the believers that "our struggle is not against flesh and blood [people]" but against spiritual forces (verse 12)? It is because he had just finished admonishing the saints in Ephesus and teaching them how to get along in church (chapter 4), in the home (chapters 5 and 6), and in the workplace (chapter 6).

Those primary relationships of Christian to Christian, husband to wife, wife to husband, child to parent, parent to child, employee to employer, and employer to employee are the main staging areas for friendly fire! And Paul wanted to make sure we were shooting at the enemy, not at each other!

Have we listened? Not very well.

After more than 20 years of serving God's people, one of the most difficult and disheartening challenges we have had to face has been attacks from those working alongside us. Therefore, we have come to realize that the interpersonal conflicts we experience within our own ranks form the central theater for operations for spiritual warfare.

Satan's primary tactics are discouragement, dissension, and division. He seeks to search and destroy through a "divide and conquer" strategy. If he can find a way to drive wedges between God's people, he can tempt us to turn our fire on one another. And the consequences and collateral damage from these internal conflicts can be devastating.

Dealing with Injuries from Friendly Fire

Conflict, confrontation, forgiveness, and reconciliation are among the most critical issues within the church today. Since interpersonal conflicts—friendly fire—can strike a knockout blow to any relationship, family, church, or Christian organization, it is imperative that we grow up and learn to speak the truth in love with one another (Ephesians 4:15).

Conflict and confrontation are usually perceived as "dirty words" in Christian circles—and understandably so, since few believers know how to fight fair. However, conflict is inevitable in a fallen world, and Jesus loves us anyway, even when we choose to have conflicts. We need not fear conflict. In fact, if handled properly, it can be God's operating table for correction, healing, and growth in our lives.

Confrontation, on the other hand, presents much more of a challenge to us: to walk in the light, speak the truth in love, and seek to resolve our differences before they escalate into injustices. Although forgiveness is commanded and is always a possibility, reconciliation may not be. Scripture outlines the attitude we need:

> Be of the same mind toward one another; do not be haughty in mind, but associate with the lowly. Do not be wise in your own estimation. Never pay back evil for evil to anyone. Respect what is right in the sight of all men. If possible, so far as it depends on you, be at peace with all men (Romans 12:16-18).

When we realize that we have hurt another brother or sister in Christ and that the other person is holding something against us, we cannot worship God until we try to make that relationship right. Matthew 5:23-24 instructs us to drop what we're doing in terms of our offerings to God and go get things straightened out. Where there is humility and the yearning on both sides for truthful peace, reconciliation can indeed happen. But just as it takes two to fight, it takes two to be friends. And reconciliation cannot happen unless both sides make the choice to forgive.

The good news is that, even if the other party refuses to forgive and continues to fire shots, we can still walk in freedom through forgiveness. Forgiveness is making the choice to cancel out the items in the debit column of relationships, no matter how many offenses are itemized there (Matthew 18:22). It is canceling the debts that others owe us because of their attacks or negligence and choosing not to make them pay. It is letting them off our hook and leaving all revenge and retribution in the hands of a just, wise, and merciful God (Romans 12:19).

When we make that choice to forgive, while being honest with God about how we have been hurt, then He moves in with His healing hand to begin to bandage up our wounds. If we persist in our anger, resentment, and unforgiveness, our hurt will turn to bitterness and tear us up on the inside (see Matthew 18:32-35), poisoning others through our hateful words (see Hebrews 12:15).

The bottom line is that we can put a stop to our part in friendly fire by forgiving from the heart. And by so doing, we deal a powerful blow to the enemy of our souls.

The "Non-Negotiables"

In conclusion, I want to briefly describe some very important relational "non-negotiables" that, if adhered to, will prevent much of our wounding one another. I realize that we can hurt one another unintentionally at times, but if we commit ourselves to go by the Book, as follows, there will be far fewer casualties from friendly fire.

- **Love**—When Jesus instructed His disciples in the upper room before His crucifixion, He described a relationship between His followers that would be characterized by love: "A new commandment I give to you, that you love one another. By this all men will know that you are My disciples, if you have love for one another" (John 13:34-35). First Corinthians 13 describes what love looks like and will enable you to recognize when God's *agape* love is operating in and through your life.

- **Commitment**—We must be committed to encouraging one another, helping each other succeed in our calling, and speaking well of one another. Paul affirmed the believers in Thessalonica and exhorted them to "encourage one another and build up one another, just as you also are doing" (1 Thessalonians 5:11).

- **Loyalty**—No person in a leadership role, whether he be husband, father, pastor, missionary, or business leader, can survive disloyalty—especially when it comes from those closest to us. One of the enemy's favorite tactics to discourage us is gossip and attacks against our character and reputation. Loyalty does not mean blind obedience; there should always be room for discussion and disagreement. Rather, loyalty means we are faithful to the other person, desiring and seeking with all our heart to make him or her successful.

- **Respect**—Everyone deserves our respect, no matter what their rank or position might be, because every person has been created in the image and likeness of God. Therefore, respect for others as people is not something they must earn. It must be granted even to those whose *behavior* is not worthy of respect. We must "*honor all people*, love the brotherhood, fear God, honor the king" (1 Peter 2:17).

These first four values of love, commitment, loyalty, and respect are not optional, no matter what others have done to us. During my years in the army, every soldier I served with realized that we had to abide by these four values whether we liked it or not. However, in the heat of battle, where the metal meets the meat, the fifth value was absolutely essential for our very survival. It is the glue that holds armies—including the army of God—together.

- **Trust**—We can respect people even when they have hurt us badly, though we will likely no longer trust them. Respect is one of the non-negotiables, but trust must be earned. If there is a breach of trust, it will take time to repair, and in some cases trust may never be fully restored. If there is no trust, we may work together to accomplish some common goal or objective, but there can be no lasting, meaningful relationship.

It is important to realize that God is committed to relationships in the body of Christ. Loving, caring, honest, supportive relationships. He is not and never will be satisfied with believers simply living in some kind of peaceful coexistence—declaring a cease-fire of sorts, but without any heart connection.

First Peter 1:22 makes God's objective clear, raising the bar high:

Since you have in obedience to the truth purified your souls for a sincere love of the brethren, fervently love one another from the heart.

By the grace of God and the power of the Holy Spirit, we can do just that. And when we do, the unbelieving world will finally wake up and take notice that Jesus is for real.

Dear heavenly Father, Your Word says I can have all kinds of supernatural gifts from You and even make enormous sacrifices for Your kingdom, but if I don't have love it profits me nothing and I myself am nothing. I confess the times I have placed a higher premium on being in control or "right" and have ignored Your command to love as You love. I acknowledge any hostile attitudes, slanderous words, or angry actions that have damaged other brothers or sisters in Christ. I receive Your forgiveness for these things.

Show me the people I need to go to, to be reconciled with, Lord. Remind me when I am hurt or frustrated or embarrassed or humiliated that my struggle is not against other people, but against the devil. I choose to forgive those who have hurt me and instead of attacking them, I want to aim my artillery fire at Satan and his forces. Thank You that I can make a difference for Your kingdom by speaking the truth in love and being part of Your building crew rather than Satan's wrecking crew. By Your grace and strength alone can I do this as I pray in Jesus' name, amen.

For more Scripture study on love:

Spend a day or two praying about and thinking on the truths of 1 Corinthians 13.

Questions for reflection and discussion:

Are you discouraged, disheartened, or even disillusioned with the church or serving God because of "friendly fire"? In light of this chapter, what do you think you need to do?

As we've seen here, pastors and other Christian leaders can suffer terribly from the pain caused by often well-meaning but misguided people. Take a moment and pray for your pastor or church leaders and ask the Lord what He wants to have you do this week to encourage him or them.

What does it mean to forgive? Is there anyone that has hurt you that you need to forgive, including perhaps yourself? Ask the Lord to show you who you need to forgive and make the choice to do so today. Perhaps this sample prayer may be helpful for you:

> *Dear Father, I choose to forgive (<u>name</u>) for (<u>tell God specifically what was done to you</u>) even though it made me feel (<u>express the pain of how you've been hurt</u>).*

Stay with each person the Lord brings to your mind until you can't think of anything else to forgive him or her for, then move on to the next person you need to forgive.

Do you agree that the four values of love, commitment, loyalty, and respect are relational "non-negotiables"? How are you doing in reflecting those values to the people at home, at work, in church, and in your community?

9
The Wall

It was December 16, 1969. The night was very dark as we resupplied ambush patrols in the northwestern corner of South Vietnam, near the Cambodian border. I had just left a landing zone and was heading back to base camp to refuel and pick up more supplies for our troops in the field.

As we cleared the tree line, another helicopter from our unit prepared to land in this same LZ. It was heavy with supplies, and with the night hot and humid, landing was even more challenging. Because of the danger of enemy fire, their landing lights were not turned on until the last possible instant, making it extremely difficult to judge the approach speed and altitude.

Knowing how difficult it had been for me to execute our landing into an area about the size of a house in the middle of this tropical rain forest, I banked my aircraft to check on the other chopper. I was aware they were short on their final approach because I was talking with them over the radio. As I circled back again over the LZ and gained altitude as quickly as possible, everything seemed under control.

All of a sudden I saw the explosion below me.

No one will ever know exactly what had happened in those few seconds previous. All I cared was that my friends had just crashed into the LZ. Their fuel bladders had ruptured and the explosion and fire were enormous.

We landed immediately, within about 50 yards of their position. The heat from the crash was too intense to get any closer. As we touched down, I could see the crew desperately trying to escape the burning inferno in which they were trapped.

I ordered my crew chief to lock and load his M-16, leave our helicopter, and try to rescue our friends. I kept my gunner behind his M-60 to give us covering fire if we needed it. I wanted so badly to unstrap my shoulder harness and run to their aid, but I had to remain behind the controls. I felt helpless.

To our amazement, I watched my friend "Sugi" get out of the cockpit and start walking toward us. He was a human torch—his entire body was on flames. As soon as my crew chief reached him, he rolled him in the grass to put out the fire. I never expected Sugi to get back up, but he did.

The crew chief tried desperately to get to the other three crew members in the burning aircraft. Meanwhile, Sugi kept walking toward us. When he reached our helicopter, I could already smell his burning flesh. His flight suit and helmet had melted into his body. I couldn't believe he was still alive. He climbed into the back cargo bay and sat down. When our crew chief returned, we took off and headed south to the burn unit in Saigon, 30 minutes away. There would be no adequate help for Sugi at our base-camp hospital.

I never reached more than 300 feet of altitude as I pushed my cyclic stick forward to maximum speed. We hit the landing pad in Saigon in record time, and Sugi just stepped off the helicopter and walked away. I would never see him again. He died minutes later.

That day two friends and fellow pilots of mine, Warrant Officer Michael Joseph Drake and Warrant Officer Leonard James Sugimoto, died. They had been flying that mission together. As pilots and friends, we would have done anything to help one another. I had flown missions with both these men.

Sugi was aircraft commander and I was flying right seat with him the night our engine quit over the Michelin Rubber Plantation. I am convinced I wouldn't be writing this book had he not been with me that night when God answered the prayers of two women back in Illinois.

Len Sugimoto was one of the best pilots I ever flew with. He perished just five weeks shy of his twenty-third birthday. Another pilot who knew Sugi posted this note on the Vietnam Veterans Memorial Page Web site just two years ago, and I found what he wrote as I was researching this information:

> Len Sugimoto was a fine pilot and officer. I went to flight school with Len and I remember him vividly. He was quick and athletic, and a superb pilot. His quiet sense of humor was always just below the surface. He married just at the end of flight school as I did, and he moved off post into temporary housing—in a trailer as I remember. All of us newlyweds swapped stories of the trials of mixing flight school and a new marriage! Len volunteered to do a difficult job when his country called, and he did it the best he knew how. No country could ask more than Len gave.[32]

In 1994, Kathy and I had our hands full planting a bilingual church in Miami, Florida. We had never visited out nation's capital, and we decided it would be a good time to do so because our youngest daughter, Sarah, needed to do a field trip as a high-school requirement. I really didn't put much thought into the trip, nor was I thinking about what we might see.

We arrived in Washington, DC, late on a March night. It was approaching midnight and traffic was light, so we decided to drive around the White House and the Constitution Gardens to see the Washington Monument and the Lincoln Memorial. Parking spaces were plentiful, so we stopped and walked into the park.

I had always wanted to see the Vietnam Veterans Memorial, or "The Wall" as it is now referred to. In order to construct it, a 500-foot slice was taken out of the ground in the middle of the park. The memorial consists of two walls, with the east one pointing to the Washington Monument and the west one pointing toward the Lincoln Memorial.

The material chosen for the memorial was black granite. When carved the rock turns white—which allows the 58,235 names of those who lost their lives in Vietnam to stand out boldly. The granite is so highly polished that it acts as an almost perfect mirror. As you stand in front of it in the sunshine, you see your image reflected back. It is a stark reminder that though the names of the dead are engraved on the wall, we—on this side of life—cannot reach them and they cannot reach us.

If you have never been to this place, it is not easy to find—even in daylight. We approached from the north side and didn't see the memorial until we were on top of it. I started along the walkway in front of the Wall. I soon noticed the flowers, pictures, cards, and personal items left in front of the many panels by relatives and friends.

As I reached the dividing point between the east and west walls, I stepped back onto the grassy knoll behind me, and sat down. Gazing at the memorial, my emotions hit like a runaway truck and overwhelmed me. I began to weep uncontrollably.

Both Kathy and Sarah came over and just held me. The woman who had waited until I came home from the war to marry me, and my youngest daughter—born to us ten years later—were now comforting their husband and father. Neither of them said a word. But they understood that a soldier had come home, and my girls were there when I needed them.

After a while, Kathy and Sarah left me alone to look at the names of my fallen friends, like Sugi…and to remember.

Sarah's recollections of that night are poignant and profoundly meaningful to me:

The dark shadow of the Wall swallowed my sight as I searched for my father's silhouette. The myriad engraved names moaned with memories of the soldiers' souls. They told of terror and triumph, death and duty, suffering and salvation. Drizzles of rain dampened my pencil and paper as I reached the place on the Wall where my father had found the names of his friends. Each engraved letter loaded me down with more awareness of my missing link to this father of mine.

Trembling, my dad turned to hold me, but to my astonishment it was not him. Facing me was a 19-year-old boy who had seen horrors no human can fathom. Tears that I had never seen him shed before poured down, dropping him to his knees. So overwhelming was his grief that I didn't know what to do or say to comfort him. So I proceeded to trace the name of the man who had burned to death before my helpless father's eyes.

While each letter lifted onto the paper, the understanding dripped into my conscious mind. The reflection of the names rippled, revealing the reason for rejoicing: I was not replicating my father's name. I looked in awe at this man who had attempted to provide—and to protect what he felt was true. I began to grasp what he had lost in order to fight. I had seen him as a carpenter, missionary, pastor, leader, speaker, and teacher. Now I could say I knew him not only as a spiritual soldier, but as a veteran of a war that I would never understand.

I am so proud to have a father and friend who has survived and surmounted the Vietnam war. That was his boot camp for the spiritual war he now fights daily. I praise the Lord who gave me my father and who promises us victory in this life and immortality in the one to come.

Thank you, Dad. I had a hard time finding the right words to express myself. I am sure you had it a million times harder. I am so glad you are alive and strong, inside and out. I love you so much and am proud to be your daughter.

—Sarah

Though movies can portray moments of glory in battle, war is not glorious. It is brutal, cruel, painful, and bloody. More than 30 years later, I am still healing from the wounds it inflicted on my young soul. Do I regret having gone? No. It was my duty to go, and I am proud that I could serve my country. But it's a fact of life that freedom always comes with a cost, and that cost is shed blood.

The Cost of Gaining Freedom

Spiritual warfare is no different. It is not glamorous to engage the powers of darkness in seeking to rescue souls from sin and Satan. It can be very exhausting and at times dangerous work, especially as we seek to make inroads with the gospel to unreached and sometimes hostile peoples. But we should not be surprised. Our Lord Jesus Himself shed His precious blood on the cross so we could be free from the tyranny of sin, Satan, and death. Hebrews 12:3-4 exhorts us to

> consider Him who has endured such hostility by sinners against Himself, so that you will not grow weary and lose heart. You have not yet resisted to the point of shedding blood in your striving against sin.

In America right now that is true. Although some have suffered the loss of relationships, finances, jobs, and reputations for their faith, present-day Americans are not having to spill their blood for the sake of Christ, at least not yet. But countless others since the birth of the Christian faith have. After just a few short minutes of thumbing through *Foxe's Book of Martyrs* you begin to get a picture of the awful persecution and barbaric atrocities perpetrated against the saints throughout history. Such persecution continues unrelentingly today in places such as Saudi Arabia, Iran, North Korea, Vietnam, and China.

A recent report from "Voice of the Martyrs" (VOM) is tragically typical of what still goes on:

> Chinese Christian Zhang Yi-nan was badly beaten by fellow inmates [his] first day as an inmate at the "re-education through

labor" facility where he is serving a two-year sentence [for his Christian faith]. A sympathetic official at the camp revealed this information to VOM sources inside China. Zhang was beaten by fellow inmates at the behest of prison guards, who considered the beating to be "Lesson One" in his so-called "re-education." "Zhang Yi-nan is a strong man," said the official, "but he was terribly beaten. His hands were bleeding badly."

Other sources inside China have confirmed the death of Chinese Christian Zhang Hong-mei. Hong-mei, a 33-year-old woman, was arrested...by local police in...Shandong Province. At 2 pm on the day of her arrest, her family was called by police and told to pay a bribe of 3,000 RMB (about $400 US). The family couldn't raise that money, so at 7 pm Hong-mei's husband, Xu Feng-hai, and her brother went to the PSB station to request her release. They saw her, bound with heavy chains to the so-called "tiger bench." She was visibly wounded, and could not speak to them.

The following afternoon the family was called to the station, where they were told that Hong-mei had died that day at noon. An autopsy showed numerous wounds to her face, hands and leg, and serious internal bleeding. "Our hearts go out to this family," said [VOM spokesman Todd] Nettleton. "We join them in asking for an investigation into this incident. We also thank God for the example of Chinese Christians like Zhang Hong-mei, who are ready to die rather than deny their faith in Christ."[33]

What should be our response to such injustice? To decry it and fight for justice, of course! But what should our response be to such persecution should it happen to us?

Perhaps one of the most eloquent, well-known, and authoritative voices on the persecution of believers is the Reverend Josef Tson. Tson has served as President of the Romanian Missionary Society since 1982 and is pastor of the Baptist church in Brasov, Romania. In 1974 he was arrested, beaten, imprisoned, and relentlessly interrogated under the cruel totalitarian regime of Nicolae Ceaușescu. Eventually, Tson was exiled from Romania in 1981, but was able to return to his newly liberated homeland in 1991.[34]

How to Face Persecution

Reverend Tson teaches a few very simple yet profound principles that he learned the hard way—in the midst of intense battle. His words are tried, true, and very relevant today in America as we face the present threat of terrorism and the future possibility of more severe persecution.

First, we need to *grab hold of and not let go of the truth that our lives "are hidden with Christ in God."* As Reverend Tson said, "To get to me, they had to go through Jesus and the Father first."[35] That is a place of great security: knowing that no one can touch us unless God allows it—and that what He allows, He will give grace to endure.

Second, and building on the first point, we need to *rest in the sovereignty of God.* Tson's definition of sovereignty is this: God is so much in charge of what is happening that in the end He uses all His enemies' schemes for His great purposes.[36]

After Tson spoke at Southern Baptist Theological Seminary in Louisville, Kentucky, a Christian news magazine reported,

> Christians under persecution should realize that God is absolutely sovereign and in control of all the affairs of his people, Tson said. "When I was in prison it was like seeing my God moving his six puppet strings," he said, referring to the six guards charged with his interrogation. "That's understanding sovereignty. Look to them [persecutions] as God's puppet strings for you. They are his instruments for you."[37]

Third, we must *learn to live by the principle of Romans 12:21—"Do not be overcome by evil, but overcome evil with good."* Tson teaches that love, not evil, is the aggressor. When being interrogated by the cruelest investigator in all of Romania, he told the man repeatedly that he was praying for him. When the weeks of interrogation were finally over, the man told Josef he would miss him! It was a moment of supreme triumph for Christ and His servant. Truly, (God's) love *never* fails (1 Corinthians 13:8).

Fourth, we need to *understand that suffering produces glory.* The apostle Paul, a man who suffered much for the kingdom of God, explained this:

> *The Spirit Himself testifies with our spirit that we are children of God, and if children, heirs also, heirs of God and fellow heirs with Christ, if indeed we suffer with Him so that we may also be glorified with Him. For I consider that the sufferings of this present time are not worthy to be compared with the glory that is to be revealed to us* (Romans 8:16-18)...*for momentary, light affliction is producing for us an eternal weight of glory far beyond all comparison* (2 Corinthians 4:17).

These words and concepts above are, by and large, strangers to us here in America, where we have enjoyed such freedom of religion. But they were anchors of hope to Josef Tson during the days of his incarceration.

He had come to see that, just as Jesus was the Lamb led to the slaughter, so are we placed in this world as helpless sheep before wolves (Matthew 10:16). What hope of victory is there in such a position? Only this: that our protecting Shepherd will never leave us and that, if He should choose to allow us to suffer or even die, God will gain glory and His kingdom will advance.

At one point during Reverend Tson's imprisonment, things were getting to the point where he was in grave danger of losing his life. His books and tapes were all over Romania by this time, and his life and work posed a great threat to the Communist regime.

But God had prepared Josef Tson for such a time as this. He told his interrogators, "Let me tell you how this works. Your greatest weapon is to kill me. My greatest weapon is to die. If you put me to death, my blood will be sprinkled over every one of my books and tapes and they will become ten times more powerful than they are now."

There is no way to defeat such a man!

As Tson has said, "The most dangerous man is the one who is not afraid to die."[38] The terrorists have learned and applied that principle for evil. Isn't it time for believers in Christ to live by that principle for good?

In the book of Revelation, Jesus predicted that some of His people would suffer greatly for His kingdom. His counsel to them should be taken by us as well when we face persecution:

> Do not fear what you are about to suffer. Behold, the devil is about to cast some of you into prison, so that you will be tested, and you will have tribulation for ten days. Be faithful until death, and I will give you the crown of life (Revelation 2:10).

As the age draws to a close and Jesus' appearing draws near, the spiritual battle will be won only at great cost—the laying down of lives for the sake of Christ. But the victories that will result will be so decisive that the power of Satan himself will be overcome, as the "voice in heaven" in Revelation 12:10-11 assures us:

> Now the salvation, and the power, and the kingdom of our God and the authority of His Christ have come, for the accuser of our brethren has been thrown down, he who accuses them before our God day and night. And they overcame him because of the blood of the Lamb and because of the word of their testimony, and they did not love their life even when faced with death.

In America the time will come when courage will be a daily requirement for those who name the Name of Christ, "but the people who know their God will display strength and take action" (Daniel 11:32).

One of the devil's greatest weapons is fear. He wants us to believe that our situations are pointless and that we are helpless, hopeless, and alone. But this is not a time to cower in fear and unbelief, for God is with us. Take hold of these encouraging words from the apostle Paul:

God has not given us a spirit of timidity, but of power and love and discipline. Therefore do not be ashamed of the testimony of our Lord or of me His prisoner, but join with me in suffering for the gospel according to the power of God (2 Timothy 1:7-8).

You can count on it. The clash between light and darkness will bring events that will cause many to cave in to fear and anxiety. Terrorists will seek to bring free nations to their knees. Unrest will destabilize governments. Religious liberties will erode. Cult leaders will take advantage of confusion to provide counterfeit answers. Even believers will be hard-pressed to resist panic and walk in peace.

For Christian men and women, this situation will be a fork in the road—where the choice will be to either stand strong or shrink back. The time to make the decision to stand is not when persecution arrives, but *now*.

Be on the alert, stand firm in the faith, act like men, be strong. Let all that you do be done in love (1 Corinthians 16:13-14).

Dear heavenly Father, we have enjoyed such freedoms in our nation for so long that we are all tempted to take them for granted and complacently believe they will always be ours. We acknowledge our presumption. We confess we have forgotten the price that has been paid by brave men throughout our history who have fought and died for these freedoms. We thank You for Your gift of forgiveness through Christ.

Open our eyes to the ways the heart and soul of our nation and its precious liberties are already being eroded under us. And give us courage to stand and fight for truth and justice in the name and by the power of the Lord Jesus Christ. And should we or our children or our grandchildren be faced with the choice to renounce our faith and live or stand firm and die, then grant them and us grace and the strength of heart at that moment to take up our cross and follow Christ. Thank You that the momentary, light afflictions we may suffer are and will be producing in

*us an eternal weight of glory. In the name of our courageous
and humble Lord Jesus we pray, amen.*

For further Scripture study
on suffering:

Take a prayer walk through the Hall of Faith, found in
Hebrews 11.

Questions for reflection and discussion:

What was your reaction when you read Reverend Josef
Tson's story of confident faith, courage, and love in the
midst of persecution?

As you look over Tson's four principles for victory under
persecution, what is the Lord saying to you in regard to
your own life and what you need Him to work on?

Hebrews 13:3 says, "Remember the prisoners, as though
in prison with them, and those who are ill-treated, since
you yourselves also are in the body." In light of this scripture and the needs of our persecuted brothers and sisters
around the world, what might you or your church do?

What decision(s) do you need to make today to stand up
for Christ in your present circumstances, as well as prepare for the day of more severe testing?

10
Welcome Home, Soldier

I returned to America from Vietnam in September 1970, one year to the day I first set foot on foreign soil as a new soldier entering combat. We came through a military processing station at San Francisco International Airport, where we changed from our grubby combat flight suits into our dress uniforms after a grueling nonstop flight from Saigon. None of us had slept on the flight. We were too excited about coming home to see our families.

As soon as we arrived at the main terminal, I sensed something was very wrong. People were looking at me strangely...almost with disdain. Here I was in my officer's uniform with a chest full of medals, and yet people seemed to be avoiding me. Still, I had a smile on my face and a spring in my step. I was going home. I had survived.

I needed to fly to Chicago's O'Hare Airport to meet my family, so I hurried to the ticket counter to make connections. Approaching the line, I greeted those around me and told them how happy I was to be home, safe and secure. I couldn't wait to get on the plane.

As I waited for my turn at the counter, I could hear people mumbling derogatory remarks about our soldiers' involvement in the Vietnam conflict. I turned around to ask them about their concerns. A young man and his wife looked me right in the eyes and called me a "baby killer."

I was stunned. I had no words to reply. At that moment every ounce of joy, pride, energy, and courage left in my soul drained out of me. I thought to myself, *Wasn't it for you that I went to fight?*

Perhaps I had been naïve in thinking that the greatest love a man could show for his country was his willingness to lay down his life for the downtrodden—whether they spoke English or Vietnamese. If I had had civilian clothes in my bag, I would have changed into them immediately before getting on the plane. I felt rejected and ashamed.

When I arrived in Chicago, my whole family was there to greet me. By now, though, I was so tired and disillusioned that I could hardly enjoy their welcome. It was as if I were in some kind of time warp. I could hardly take in what they were saying to me, and their words only ricocheted off my heart. Still, it was great to see them—my wonderful parents and ten younger brothers and sisters (all of whom are still alive as I write these words—this chapter is dedicated to them).

Arriving at our house, I got out of my uniform right away and took a hot bath for the first time in more than a year. I put on some old clothes because I yearned to settle back into familiar surroundings and pretend I had never left home. I was skin and bones, and suffering physically from my tour of duty in Southeast Asia. My mom, who is a nurse, fretted over me, crying that night because she didn't know how to help her firstborn son.

That night I lay down in my old bed and slept soundly well into the next day. I was exhausted physically, mentally, and emotionally, and empty spiritually. A son and brother who had left as a starry-eyed 18-year-old boy was home again. But I was not the same man. I was confused, bitter, and broken.

After World War II, veterans had the time and opportunity to process what they had gone through during their years of combat in that global conflict—a war in which the lines between good and evil were more clearly drawn. Most of them returned on ships that could take a month or more to reach our shores. But in the case of the Vietnam conflict, one night you could be flying a helicopter gunship mission over the steamy Mekong Delta, and 48 hours later you could be back on the streets of your hometown. The transitional shock was enormous.

I remember dropping in on friends after returning home, trying to reconnect with them. They'd ask me, "Where have you been? I haven't seen you for a while." They spoke as if I'd been gone only a few weeks. I would usually respond, "I was in Nam for the last year."

But as soon as I started to talk about what it was like, they would change the subject. They didn't want to hear about it. My family, friends, and even my country were not willing or able to help me make the transition from soldier to civilian.

I had been flying combat missions in Vietnam on May 4, 1970, when our own National Guard soldiers were called to the campus of Kent State University in Ohio to quell the antiwar demonstrations being held there. When it was all over, four young students lay dead, and ten others were wounded. That was a tragic moment in our nation's history for all Americans, no matter what side of the controversy they were on.

It is one of our most precious freedoms that gave people the right to protest the war in Vietnam, and still gives us the right to protest any other war for that matter. What concerns me is that during and after Vietnam, the American people abused that freedom. Going beyond their right to protest the war effort, many of them leveled their attacks against the warriors sent into that war. And that was terribly wrong.

Twenty-two years after I returned from Vietnam, Kathy and I were church planting among the Cuban population of Miami, Florida. We had established several bilingual cell groups in our neighborhood in western Dade County. (We were among the few "gringos" living in this fast-growing area.)

That week in 1992, we were preparing to launch our first Sunday-morning services in the ballroom on the campus of Florida International University near our home. The county fair is held on this campus each year, and we attended on Saturday.

It was your typical county fair. There were carnival rides, 4-H displays, hawkers at their booths selling anything and everything, and displays set up by a variety of local, county, and state governmental organizations. The air was filled with noise, laughter, and shouting in several different languages. It was sort of an organized chaos of good times and good smells.

Kathy and I strolled comfortably through the displays, sampling the different foods and purchasing all the unnecessary stuff that later ends up in garage sales. Kathy walked on ahead of me when something caught my eye. I had noticed a canvas wall full of pictures and several tables set up with military paraphernalia from the Vietnam conflict.

I stopped to examine the memorabilia from an era in my life that I thought was long since over. As I stood there, I was captured by the items on the table, which took me back to the sights and sounds of war. Looking up, I noticed a man and woman standing behind the display booth watching me. They must have observed my interest in their display.

While I was engrossed in the objects on display, absorbed in memories of war, the couple walked up to the table, stood in front of me, and said hello. Having caught my attention, they looked me in the eye and said together, "Welcome home, soldier."

It was as if they had pulled out a .45-caliber handgun and shot me in the chest. I dropped to my knees and began to sob uncontrollably. I had never heard anyone say that to me even though I had risked everything in Vietnam. I didn't know that there were so many bottled-up emotions inside of me…but they knew.

I had learned to "stuff" it all.

Their words broke an emotional dam I had built over the years to protect myself from all of war's painful experiences. Pain that I had never shared with anyone, not even my wife.

I now found myself on the floor in front of their display booth crying like a baby. People walking by thought I was crazy, but I didn't care. Tears of healing were flowing freely down my face. I looked up and caught sight of Kathy turning around to see where I had gone.

She immediately came running to my side, not understanding what had just happened. I think she thought someone had hurt me.

Through my sobs I told her what had just happened. She lifted me to my feet and held me. It was one of the sweetest moments and hugs, something I'll remember forever. She didn't say anything. She didn't have to. I knew she understood. She had lived with me through so many years of the nightmares and fallout in my life from my time as a young soldier.

She thanked the couple and led me down the sawdust path of the fairgrounds, out into the fresh air. We sat on a bench together and she held me and let me cry.

~

In June of 1991 our troops returned home from the first Gulf War in Iraq. They were met with a ticker-tape victory parade in our nation's capital. I remember turning on the news channel and watching them ride down our city streets, celebrating and being cheered on by the majority of Americans and the news media. It was an emotional catharsis for most of us, especially Vietnam veterans. For me personally, it was a magical moment that helped lift me out of my post-Vietnam trauma…for our nation did not say "thank you" or give us this kind of recognition. I relished and identified with the enthusiasm and joy of our troops that day as we welcomed them home. It was as if I were riding in the parade with them.

Looking Ahead to Home

Child of God, you may never be thanked, honored, or applauded on planet Earth for your service to the King in this spiritual war. Instead, you may even be called all kinds of names and be treated with cruelty and contempt. But take courage! One day Jesus will personally see to it that you are safe in His arms, because you'll be home. In Revelation 7:9-17, John records his vision of such a moment:

I looked, and behold, a great multitude which no one could count, from every nation and all tribes and peoples and tongues, standing before the throne and before the Lamb, clothed in white robes, and palm branches were in their hands; and they cry out with a loud voice, saying,

"Salvation to our God who sits on the throne, and to the Lamb." And all the angels were standing around the throne and around the elders and the four living creatures; and they fell on their faces before the throne and worshiped God, saying,

"Amen, blessing and glory and wisdom and thanksgiving and honor and power and might, be to our God forever and ever. Amen."

Then one of the elders answered, saying to me, "These who are clothed in the white robes, who are they, and where have they come from?" I said to him, "My lord, you know." And he said to me, "These are the ones who come out of the great tribulation, and they have washed their robes and made them white in the blood of the Lamb. For this reason, they are before the throne of God; and they serve Him day and night in His temple; and He who sits on the throne will spread His tabernacle over them. They will hunger no longer, nor thirst anymore; nor will the sun beat down on them, nor any heat; for the Lamb in the center of the throne will be their shepherd, and will guide them to springs of the water of life; and God will wipe every tear from their eyes."

And again, in Revelation 21:3-7:

And I heard a loud voice from the throne, saying, "Behold, the tabernacle of God is among men, and He will dwell among them, and they shall be His people, and God Himself will be among them, and He will wipe away every tear from their eyes; and there will no longer be any death; there will no longer be any mourning, or crying, or pain; the first things have passed away."

And He who sits on the throne said, "Behold, I am making all things new." And He said, "Write, for these words are faithful and true." Then He said to me, "It is done. I am the Alpha and the Omega, the beginning and the end. I will give to the one who thirsts from the spring of the water of life without cost. He who overcomes will inherit these things, and I will be his God and he will be My son."

None of us knows the day or the hour that Christ will split the skies and return like the lightning flashing from the east to the west (Matthew 24:27). Then it will all be over. There will be no more spiritual battles. No more opportunities for heroism in the kingdom of God. The judgment will come. Time will be no more. And rewards will be granted by the King to His servants.

There will be the *crown of life* for those who have been approved by the Lord as having persevered under trial (James 1:12). There will be the *imperishable wreath* to those who, in exercising self-control, have run the race and fought the fight to win (1 Corinthians 9:24-27). There will be the *crown of exultation* for those who have invested their lives in others for the kingdom of God (1 Thessalonians 2:19-20). There will be the *crown of righteousness* that the Lord Jesus will award to all who have loved His appearing (2 Timothy 4:8). And there will be the *crown of glory* for faithful shepherds who have served under the Chief Shepherd (1 Peter 5:2-4).

Though the judgment for our sins has fully fallen on Christ, so that all who trust in Him alone to save them are forever forgiven, there remains yet a judgment for our works. The warrior Paul the apostle wrote of this:

According to the grace of God which was given to me, like a wise master builder I laid a foundation, and another is building on it. But each man must be careful how he builds on it. For no man can lay a foundation other than the one which is laid, which is Jesus Christ. Now if any man builds on the foundation with gold, silver, precious stones, wood, hay, straw, each man's work will become evident; for the day will show it because it is to be revealed with fire, and the fire itself will test the quality of each man's work. If any man's work which he has built on it remains, he will receive a reward. If any man's work is burned up, he will suffer loss; but he himself will be saved, yet so as through fire (1 Corinthians 3:10-15).

It's not too late. Even if you have not run the race well or fought the good fight so far, you can start over today. Don't wait. *Today,* if you hear God speaking to you, it is time to enlist, as Paul urged: "Suffer hardship with me, as a good soldier of Christ Jesus. No soldier in active service entangles himself in the affairs of everyday life, so that he may please the one who enlisted him as a soldier" (2 Timothy 2:3-4).

There is no earthly pleasure or treasure for which it is worth forfeiting the glory of seeing the Lord Jesus face-to-face, having Him wrap His arms around you and wipe away every tear, and hearing Him say, "Welcome home, soldier. Well done, good and faithful servant. Enter into the joy of your Master."

Dear heavenly Father, it is much too easy to live in light of today or even tomorrow yet forget about eternity. I confess that too often I have allowed myself to become entangled in the affairs of everyday life—living as a civilian when I'm called to be a soldier. This day, however, I hear Your voice, Your call to lay up treasures in heaven rather than accumulating stuff on earth. I hear You urging me to see others in my home, my workplace, my church, and my community in light of eternity. I need You to open my eyes to see things as You see them and live in light of the judgment of my works that is to come. I long to see my life as a huge treasure of gold, silver, and precious stones, not as a worthless pile of wood, hay, and straw. Empower me by Your Holy Spirit to live for Your glory and to run the race, finish the course, and fight the good fight of faith in this world until You call me home. In Jesus' name, amen.

For further Scripture study
on eternity:

Read anything in the book of Revelation. For a warm-up you can also read 2 Peter 3.

Questions for reflection and discussion:

When Christ judges our works in heaven, what will determine whether something is gold, silver, and precious stones—or wood, hay, and straw? (Keep in mind that God is not only interested in what you do but why and how you do it.)

The Bible says that in heaven God will wipe away every tear and there will no longer be any mourning, pain, tears, or death. In what ways are those promises particularly meaningful to you today?

What does it take to truly make the shift from comfortable civilian-living to becoming a good soldier of Christ Jesus? How can you do this while still being a joyful person who celebrates the good things in life God has given us?

Based on the reading and study of this book, what does God want you to do to reach out to others who don't know Christ and to reach into your church to help saints who are struggling? Pray and ask Him to give you His battle plan for spiritual warfare!

Epilogue
by Kathy Wasmond

Life is a journey down an unmarked path. None of us knows where it will take us with its many twists and turns. I was only 13 years old and Joe was only 14 when we first met. I was a young, starry-eyed romantic who thought our relationship would always be lined with flowering trees and sunshine.

Thirty-six years ago I watched as the man God had chosen to be my partner for life became a raw recruit in boot camp. And the 12 months he would then spend at war would end up haunting the two of us for years.

The journey I stepped out on the day I married Joe in 1970 was not one of flowering trees and sunshine. Instead, dark storm clouds rolled in, obscuring the sun. Littering our path were the bewildering, painful memories and fallout from a place in Southeast Asia, an area of the world unknown to me, called Vietnam.

There are some things we never forget. They may pass out of the front of our memory, but they are always somewhere in the back of our minds swirling around—and the least little thing forces us to recall and encounter them. The traumatic and hurtful experiences of life have a way of controlling and manipulating us, causing us to form false identities.

Insidiously, Joe's painful, embedded memories of war became a part of our mutual life together. The anguishing experiences from

Vietnam that were irremovably locked in Joe's subconscious surfaced nightly in the form of relentless, tormenting nightmares. He tried desperately to be free, but he was imprisoned by what he had seen and had had to do. He was a prisoner of war, being held captive by a mind filled with dark and unforgettable events.

What he spoke out loud during those nightmares went beyond my comprehension. Night after night I tried to comfort him, but nothing I did would stop them or even ease his troubled soul.

More than three decades have passed since those nights of terror began. Looking back, from the perspective of God's Word, it is clear now that the horrific memories from the Vietnam war were certainly one of Satan's tools designed to weaken and cripple my husband.

At that point in our lives, however, I did not understand we were in a spiritual battle. What I did know was that my sympathy and love for Joe was not sufficient. I couldn't fix him. I only wanted to be his wife. He needed something more, and someone greater than me to heal his damaged emotions. The spiritual conflict was tearing at our lives and destroying our relationship with one another. Nevertheless, we desperately wanted our marriage to work, and we both wanted it badly enough to do whatever was necessary to make it healthy.

It is clear now that one of the reasons—no doubt the main reason—we survived and grew deeper in love with each other was our encounter with the Lord Jesus Christ. The apostle Paul's words in Romans 5:6-8 still echo in my mind as I recall that bright October day in 1977 when our cry for help was answered.

Our search had led us to a pastor named Willis Reed, a retired army chaplain from World War II who is now at home with the Lord. Reverend Reed listened to our story of helplessness, and with an understanding that comes only from the Spirit of God, he lovingly read this passage to us from the Bible:

> *While we were still helpless, at the right time Christ died for the ungodly. For one will hardly die for a righteous man; though*

perhaps for the good man someone would dare even to die. But God demonstrates His own love toward us, in that while we were yet sinners, Christ died for us.

The truth of the Word of God penetrated my hungry heart, and two weeks later I came to a personal relationship with Jesus Christ. Joe, too, cried out in his brokenness and received Christ that very same day. Our journey then took a miraculous turn, one that has brought us into full-time ministry and the writing of this book.

You have read about some of the memories Joe tried so hard to forget. However, God, in His divine love, wisdom, and tender mercy has shown us both that trying to remember has worked much better than trying to forget.

The lessons I learned in the early years of our journey are still with me today. One of those is that being set free from our past may happen quickly or it may be a step-by-step process. For Joe, freedom and healing from the tormenting memories of Vietnam did not come immediately. In fact, the memories are still with him today, though the torment and fear has been replaced with freedom and faith. His memories of that time and place—some still as vivid today as the day they occurred—have been used by God so that he is now courageously sharing this message of freedom in Christ with other "prisoners of war."

We have also learned that it is what we allow God to do with our experiences that makes all the difference. You know you are healed when painful and hurtful events and experiences from your past no longer control your present or dictate who you are as a person.

As I watched my husband continue to suffer many nights—even after our conversion to biblical Christianity—I would cry out to the Lord in prayer. It was during those dark hours that I learned to fight for him when he was too weak to do battle on his own. It helps to remember that we are not only wives, but fellow soldiers in this freedom fight. Learning how to stand beside our husbands with the weapon of prayer is crucial in defeating the enemy's attempts to steal, kill, and destroy. Prayer truly is a "weapon of mass reconstruction" (see 2 Corinthians 10:3-5).

Somehow I feel I am not alone. I know that there are countless brothers and sisters in Christ who have been awakened to the reality of spiritual warfare. You are probably among them, or you wouldn't have picked up this book in the first place. Like me, you are learning how to use the weapons of warfare for the welfare of those you love, all to the glory of God.

Be encouraged! For Joe and me, the journey that began on a path littered with painful memories that could have destroyed us is now— 34 years later—a story of God's faithfulness to answer prayer and His eagerness to set other captives free.

As a woman, wife, and mother, I encourage you—no, I challenge you—to step boldly into this cosmic battle for our men. As our Cuban friends in Miami would often say to us during our time of church-planting there, "Estamos juntos aquí en la lucha." Roughly translated, this means, "We are here in the battle together."

Appendix
An Overview of the War Zone

Kathy and I had no biblical training in how to handle our daughter's night-terror experiences. Nor, at that time, did we have any idea what to think of the frightening nighttime presence I had encountered as a child. (See chapter 1.) Sadly, most Christians in America are in the same boat with such situations.

What was going on? Were my daughter and I simply victims of overactive imaginations? Were we seeing ghosts—the spirits of some poor, departed souls? Were we the victims of psychotic episodes or some other mental illness?

David Hufford, who researched night-terror experiences in several different cultures and through the literature of the last several hundred years, would have categorized my childhood experience as "being hagged." (The term is derived from Newfoundland folklore about "the Old Hag" and "nightmare."[39] The term "nightmare" literally means "night demon," referring to an evil spirit that was formerly believed to haunt and suffocate sleeping people.[40])

From his research, Hufford summarizes the night-terror experience in the following four possible elements:[41]

1. awakening (or immediately preceding sleep)

2. hearing or seeing (or both) something come into the room and approach the bed

3. being pressed on the chest or strangled

4. having the inability to move or cry out until either being brought out of the state by someone else or breaking through the feeling of paralysis on one's own.

> This experience is explained as caused by either a supernatural assault, indigestion, circulatory stagnation, or some combination of them all.

Hufford was surprised by the frequency with which this experience occurs and suggested that his own research raises the question as to how something so common can be so unknown. Without a biblical worldview or reference point, he is not quite sure what to make of his own findings. Although he would acknowledge the possibility that these night-terror experiences argue for a metaphysical reality, he concludes that "the state in which this experience occurs is probably best described as sleep paralysis with a particular kind of hypnagogic hallucination."[42]

I would agree with Hufford's hypothesis attributing some of these experiences to a known psycho-physiological state. However, without taking into account the reality of the spiritual world, his conclusions are incomplete.

A Complete Worldview

In the book *The Seduction of Our Children,* Dr. Neil Anderson gives us another perspective:

> I was conducting a conference for the leadership of one of America's flagship churches. The pastor is one of the most gifted Bible teachers I know, and his staff is among the best. I asked the 165 leaders present if they had ever experienced a direct encounter with something they knew to be demonic, such as a frightening presence in their room or an evil voice

in their mind. Ninety-five percent answered yes. I went a step further to ask how many had been frightened by something pressing on them that they couldn't immediately respond to physically. At least a third raised their hand. Are these Christian leaders mentally ill? No, and neither are your children when they struggle against demonic influences in their lives... Would you know what to do if your child was terrorized by a presence in his room? Do you fear such a possibility?[43]

This same book records the results of a survey of 1725 students (433 junior high and 1292 senior high) who attended Christian schools and camps. Half of the junior high and 47 percent of the senior high students said they had experienced a frightening presence in their room. Even among the 864 students who indicated no occult background whatsoever, the frequency of experiencing such a presence was still 40 percent.[44]

In 1992, my wife Kathy and I conducted a comparable survey in Miami, Florida, at the Christian school where she was a fourth-grade teacher. We surveyed 92 junior high and 122 senior high students. One of the questions we asked was, "Have you ever experienced some presence (seen or heard) in your room that scared you?" Our results were remarkably similar to those cited above: 46 percent of the junior high and 47 percent of the senior high students responded that they had.

In order to understand such occurrences as well as wage and win spiritual battle, we need to see the world the way God sees it. We need a biblical *worldview* that includes a healthy, balanced understanding of the spiritual realm.

In our Western culture, we have tended to believe that only what we can observe with our five senses or understand scientifically is that which is real. This rational, materialistic (dealing with the material or physical world) worldview is in direct opposition to biblical Christianity, which says that "we walk [live] by faith, not by sight" (2 Corinthians 5:7). Biblical Christianity makes it clear that beyond the physical universe there is a very real and very much active spiritual world—a world that includes not only God Himself but spiritual beings typically called demons and angels.[45]

Some cults, such as Christian Science and other so-called "mind science" groups, go to the opposite extreme. They say that the physical world is illusory and only that which is of the mind or spirit is real. (The problem with Christian Science is that it is kind of like Grape Nuts cereal. Grape Nuts is neither grapes nor nuts. Christian Science is neither Christian nor science!)

A truly biblical worldview allows for the "seen" world of God's natural creation, the "unseen" world of God Himself, and the spirit world of angels and demons. The apostle Paul did not deny the existence of the material world when he wrote, "The things which are seen are temporal, but the things which are not seen are eternal" (2 Corinthians 4:18). He was simply pointing out the fact that what we can observe with our senses today will not be around forever.

Dr. Neil Anderson and Dr. Tim Warner clearly explained and illustrated this biblical worldview in their book, *Beginner's Guide to Spiritual Warfare:*

> Biblical worldview has three functional realms: the realm of God or deity, the realm of angels and the realm of people and things. It is important to state that when we talk about these realms, we are not talking about spatial realms but realms of being. God is certainly not limited to a spatial realm far away in outer space. He is present everywhere in his creation. But God is the one being in the realm of deity—not God and angels, and certainly not God and Satan. Some Christians have such a fear of Satan that they ascribe godlike qualities to him. Some have even confessed that they see him as the counterpart of God—God being the eternal good and Satan the eternal evil. Satan isn't the eternal anything. He is a fallen angel and should never have the attributes of deity ascribed to him.[46]

The following diagram is worth a thousand words in understanding the world from a biblical point of view:

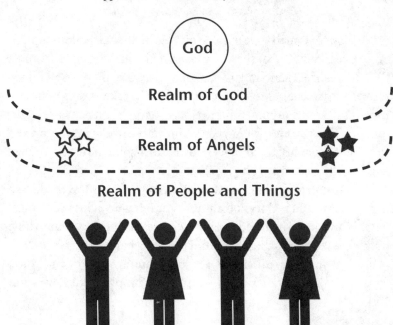

It is not necessary here to examine and try to understand the origin of the spirit world (of angels and demons). Scripture doesn't answer all our questions on this matter anyway. What is clear is that angels and demons are created spirit beings (and therefore do not have physical bodies as we do), and that they play an important role in what takes place in real time–space history on planet Earth.

Angels

In the Bible, angels worship God (see Revelation 5:11-12, for example), execute God's judgments on earth (see Revelation 8–9, for example), and bring important messages to people. An angel appeared to Zacharias, father of John the Baptist, and gave a verbal message to him (Luke 1:11-20). Mary, the mother of Jesus, also received an angelic visitation (Luke 1:26-38), as did her husband, Joseph, though his visitation was in the form of a dream (Matthew 1:20-25).

Although visual appearances of angels are not commonplace, Scripture indicates that they may be helping and serving us far more than we realize. Hebrews 1:14 says of angels, "Are they not all ministering spirits, sent out to render service for the sake of those who will inherit salvation?" Apparently angels also have the capacity to assume human form at times, for later in Hebrews we read, "Do not neglect to show hospitality to strangers, for by this some have entertained angels without knowing it" (13:2).

We are not to worship angels (see Revelation 19:10; 22:8-9), though seeing them in their glory and authority as John did in his vision must be truly awe-inspiring. God's holy angels are certainly not plump little pink-cheeked babies flitting around plucking harps! They are grand, majestic beings who are immensely powerful in strength and voice, far greater than any man. Here's just one example, from Revelation 10:1-3:

> I saw another strong angel coming down out of heaven, clothed with a cloud; and the rainbow was upon his head, and his face was like the sun, and his feet like pillars of fire; and he had in his hand a little book which was open. He placed his right foot on the sea and his left foot on the land; and he cried out with a loud voice, as when a lion roars; and when he had cried out, the seven peals of thunder uttered their voices.

There is one more function of angels that is especially pertinent to this book. They are mighty warriors, fighting against Satan and his forces (see Daniel 10 and Revelation 12:1-9, for example), engaged in a cosmic war for the hearts of men and women and the souls of nations.

Demons

So what about demons? What are they? To develop a biblical worldview of the domain of darkness, we must first shed any nonsensical image of little creatures running around in red suits with horns and pitchforks. However, neither should we adopt a mental picture of the devil or demons that makes them the opposite of God. The former picture would cause us to trivialize their existence and operation; the latter picture would move us to fear them. Either extreme would render us useless in spiritual battle.

Jesus unmasked the enemy while rebuking the unrepentant Pharisees. He said to them,

> *You are of your father the devil, and you want to do the desires of your father. He was a murderer from the beginning, and does not stand in the truth because there is no truth in him. Whenever he speaks a lie, he speaks from his own nature, for he is a liar and the father of lies* (John 8:44).

Demons are by nature cruel liars and deceivers. Because they are so adept at deception, our methodology of dealing with demonized people does not include trying to engage in conversations with demons or attempting to gain information from them about their activity. Although some in ministry do that very thing, we believe it is far safer (and in the end, far more productive) to gain information from the Spirit of truth through prayer. Why open yourself up to the very real possibility of being tricked, when you can know the truth from the source of truth Himself?

It is instructive to note that in the Gospels Jesus spends much more time telling demons to be quiet than in trying to get them to talk! Since deception is their primary modus operandi, anytime they can get a word in edgewise it puts them at an advantage.

The devil and his demons will even try to use the truth to deceive! Satan quoted Psalm 91:11-12 to Jesus in an effort to trick him (see Matthew 4:6). Of course, Jesus knew the Scriptures so well that He realized the devil was intentionally misusing the Word of God. Jesus simply quoted an appropriate truth from the book of Deuteronomy (see Matthew 4:7), and the temptation was defeated.

In my (Rich's) experience with demonized people, I have watched the enemy try to get them to fixate on certain Scriptures that bring a message of doom and gloom. One time I was encouraging a believer under spiritual attack to meditate on the very positive Psalm 145. The problem was, there is one half of one verse of that psalm that is a warning of judgment. Psalm 145:20b says, "But all the wicked He [God] will destroy." Guess which verse the enemy used against her?

Scripture is a great weapon against the enemy, but the devil will try to turn the tables on unsuspecting people by getting them to obsess over a particular Scripture, making them think God is speaking words of condemnation to them (as with the woman I mention above). Romans 8:1 says, however, that "there is now no condemnation for those who are in Christ Jesus."

The length of this book does not permit a full-scale analysis of Satan and his demons (for a more thorough examination of this topic we encourage you to read *The Bondage Breaker* by Dr. Neil Anderson and *The Adversary* and *Overcoming the Adversary* by Mark Bubeck), but we do want to follow up briefly on my (Rich's) story about Michelle's not-so-imaginary "friend" (see chapter 5). Remember that the demon identified itself as a little orphan girl named Becca who wanted to befriend my daughter?

In recent years in America there has been what we call an "angel craze." Angels have become extremely popular on TV shows, in books, in art, and in other avenues of culture. The positive side to this fad is that it reminds people that there exists an unseen spiritual world. The negative side is that without a biblical worldview to evaluate testimonies and teachings about angels, it is very easy to be deceived by the dark side.

In any matter, Scripture, not experience, must always be our plumb line to determine truth versus error. And angelic phenomena are no different.

One aspect of the current craze is the proliferation of "spirit guides" or "guardian angels" seeking to establish ongoing companionship with people. This is totally unbiblical—and any spirit being trying to gain such access to an individual is categorically demonic, no matter how sweet, kind, or wise it appears. Angels in Scripture *never* establish a friendship with a person. They come, they bring a message, and then they depart. And, with the exception of Gabriel (see Luke 1:19), holy angels *never* give their name. In only one other case is the name of a holy angel mentioned in Scripture, and his name is Michael (see Daniel 10:13; Jude 9; and others).

The problem in America today is that angels pretending to be from God are becoming guides, guards, and friends of unwary humans—and almost always they identify themselves by name! Scripture warns us,

> *And no wonder, for Satan himself masquerades as an angel of light* (2 Corinthians 11:14 NIV).

We recognize that it is easy to become frightened by the existence of such an evil spiritual reality. But as we said before, there is no place in Scripture where we are instructed to fear Satan or his demons—but we are told to be self-controlled and on the alert (see 1 Peter 5:8). "Greater is He who is in you [the Holy Spirit] than he who is in the world [the devil]" (1 John 4:4). Jesus has come to destroy the devil's works (1 John 3:8), and He has already disarmed him through the cross (Colossians 2:15-16).

Put on the full armor of God and stand firm against the enemy's schemes. Be on guard against false Christs, false spirits, and false gospels, especially as the time of Jesus' return draws near. As the apostle Paul wrote,

> *I am jealous for you with a godly jealousy. I promised you to one husband, to Christ, so that I might present you as a pure virgin to him. But I am afraid that just as Eve was deceived by the serpent's cunning, your minds may somehow be led astray from your sincere and pure devotion to Christ* (2 Corinthians 11:1-3 NIV).

Keep watching and praying lest you enter into temptation; stay close to the true and living God and His Word, and you will do well.

Acknowledgments

No one in their right mind would choose to go to war. But when I was called upon in 1968 to fight for others so they could enjoy the freedoms you and I many times take for granted, I willingly volunteered. I want to thank my parents for instilling in me the values that have served me so well over my lifetime and that have now brought me to this significant place in my life.

To my wife, Kathy, and our two lovely daughters, Jennifer and Sarah: You married and were parented by a young man who saw and experienced things no one should have to deal with. You three women, more than anyone else in my life, have endured the consequences of my time in Vietnam. Your unconditional love and acceptance along with your undying encouragement brought me through years of torment and confusion. You have all added immeasurably to my life and this book. It is as much your story as it is mine.

To Rich Miller, who co-authored this book with me: You challenged me to write—something I never intended nor desired, especially about this part of my life. You took my painful memories and helped me transform them into something that I hope will touch many lives. You were careful and sensitive with my story. You are not only my right-hand man here at Freedom in Christ Ministries, but a dear friend. I would willingly go into battle with you anywhere, at anytime.

Rich and I would also like to acknowledge the encouragement and support of Paul Gossard, our editor at Harvest House Publishers. Paul, when we initially proposed this project to you over a year ago, you saw something about it that none of us ever imagined would get this far. You have done a great job in the editorial process and have been a very significant source of encouragement to both of us.

To Tim and Eleanor Warner: We first encountered you 18 years ago, in seminary at Trinity Evangelical Divinity School in Deerfield, Illinois. Later, you mentored me through my doctoral work. More than this, you both have been role models and spiritual parents to Kathy and myself. Thank you for pouring your lives into us. You have influenced what others will read here more than you will ever know.

Ultimately, this book is my tribute to the brave soldiers I fought along-side with in Vietnam, as well as every other American who has served and is currently serving our country in military service. (And though I was, and still am, diametrically opposed to those who died by our hands, I also want to acknowledge them as brave adversaries.)

I salute you. This is your story as much as it is mine. As General Harold Moore said so well, "For we were soldiers once...and young."

Notes

1. John Eldredge, *Waking the Dead* (Nashville, TN: Thomas Nelson Publishers, 2003), p. 151.

2. C.S. Lewis, *The Screwtape Letters* (Old Tappan, NJ: Fleming H. Revell Company, 1976), p. 17.

3. Clinton Arnold, *Three Crucial Questions About Spiritual Warfare* (Grand Rapids, MI: Baker Book House, 1997), p. 19

4. U.S. Department of Defense Web site (www.dod.gov), January 2003.

5. Department of Defense Web site.

6. Timothy Warner, *Spiritual Warfare* (Wheaton, IL: Crossway Books, 1991) p. 40.

7. J. Oswald Sanders, *Spiritual Leadership* (Metro Manila, Philippines: OMF Literature, Inc., 1989), p. 106.

8. Leonard Ravenhill, *Why Revival Tarries* (Minneapolis, MN: Bethany Fellowship, Inc., 1979), p. 23.

9. Warner, p. 134.

10. John Paul Jackson, *Needless Casualties of War* (North Sutton, NH: Streams Publications, 2002), p. 44.

11. Jackson, p. 45.

12. Robert W. Martin, "The Tunnel Rats," http://www.militaryhistory.about.com/library/weekly/aa092701a., p. 1.

13. Tim Page and John Pimlott, *NAM: The Vietnam Experience 1965-1975* (Hong Kong: Orbis Publishing Ltd., 1988), p. 43.

14. Page and Pimlott, p. 71.

15. Martin, p. 2.

16. Page and Pimlott, pp. 43-44.

17. Neil Anderson and Tim Warner, *Beginner's Guide to Spiritual Warfare* (Ann Arbor, MI: Servant Publications, 2000), p. 44.

18. Anderson and Warner, p. 50.

19. "Porn in the U.S.A.," *60 Minutes* transcript, November 21, 2003.

20. "Help for Struggling Christian Leaders," www.pureintimacy.org.

21. Steve Arterburn, "Overcoming Sexual Addiction" (cassette tape) referenced on www.pureintimacy.org.

22. As quoted in "Help for Struggling Christian Leaders", www.pureintimacy.org.

23. Warner, p. 130.

24. Although we primarily present a methodology whereby believers in Christ are instructed to personally *submit to God and resist the devil* (see James 4:7), an unbeliever is incapable of exercising such authority. Therefore at times, as directed by the Holy Spirit, it may be very necessary and beneficial for another person (a Christian) to bind or cast out the demons from an unbeliever so he or she will be free to respond to the gospel and be saved. Such power encounters sometimes have provided the key to unlocking families or even people groups previously resistant to the gospel.

25. C. Peter Wagner, *Wrestling with Dark Angels* (Ventura, CA: Regal Books, 1990), p. 133.

26. Neil T. Anderson, *Victory over the Darkness* (Ventura, CA: Regal Books, 2000), pp. 16-17.

27. *The Steps to Freedom in Christ* are published as a separate volume by Gospel Light Publishers. They are also contained in the back of Dr. Anderson's book *The Bondage Breaker.* They can also be ordered online through Freedom in Christ Ministries at www.ficm.org, along with many other resources.

28. Dr. Fernando Garzon, a licensed clinical psychologist and professor at Regent University, Virginia Beach, Virginia, lists a number of advantages to using the Steps in counseling. They include "making the counselee's faith in Christ an important part of the healing process; establishing the counselee's identity and sense of worth in Christ; deepening the counselee's faith commitment; strongly connecting the Word of God with the healing process; increasing the counselee's personal responsibility in the healing process; empowering the counselee to discern truth vs. error and come against the lies; shortening the process of uncovering root issues because of its thoroughness"; and others. (Neil T. Anderson, *Discipleship Counseling* [Ventura, CA: Regal Books, 2003], p. 161-163).

29. H. Dale Burke, *Less Is More Leadership* (Eugene, OR: Harvest House Publishers, 2004), p. 15.

30. World Evangelical Fellowship newsletter, April 9, 1996, p. 1.

31. World Evangelical Fellowship newsletter.

32. Nick Lappos, www.thewall-usa.com/cgi-bin/search5.cgi, June 8, 2002. This tribute to a good man and a true hero, Leonard James "Sugi" Sugimoto, was written by and graciously permitted for use by his good friend Nick Lappos. The tribute can be accessed directly at www.thewall-usa.com.

33. Voice of the Martyrs Web site, www.persecution.com, November 11, 2003.

34. Jeff Robinson, "Persecution is coming to America, Josef Tson tells seminary students," *Worthy News,* www.worthynews.com/news-features/christian-per secution.

35. Josef Tson, message given at biennial ICBC conference, Sioux City, Iowa, March 4-6, 2004.

36. Tson.

37. Robinson.

38. Tson.

39. David Hufford, "The terror that comes by night: An experience-centered study of supernatural assault traditions" (Philadelphia: University of Pennsylvania Press, 1982), pp. 10-11.

40. *Webster's New World Dictionary of the American Language* (New York, NY: The World Publishing Company, 1968), p. 992.

41. Hufford, pp. 10-11.

42. Hufford.

43. Neil Anderson and Steve Russo, *The Seduction of Our Children* (Eugene, OR: Harvest House Publishers, 1991), pp. 26-27.

44. Anderson and Russo, pp. 34, 36.

45. We use the term *angels* in this book to identify holy spiritual beings that are under God's authority and in harmony with God and His purposes. We use it in contrast to the term *demons,* used to identify evil, unclean spiritual beings that are at cross-purposes with God. This limited use of the term *angel* should not be construed as indicating we believe that demons are not also a category of (fallen) angels. The use of the term *angel* in this limited sense is merely for simplicity and clarification.

46. Anderson and Warner, p. 69.

Books and Resources from Freedom in Christ Ministries and Neil T. Anderson

Core Message and Resources

• *The Bondage Breaker®* (Harvest House). Study guide and audiobook also available. This book explains spiritual warfare, what your protection is, ways that you are vulnerable, and how you can live a liberated life in Christ. Well over one million copies in print.

• *Victory Over the Darkness* with study guide, audiobook, and videos (Regal Books). Explains who you are in Christ, how you walk by faith, how your mind and emotions function, and how to relate to one another in Christ. Well over one million copies in print.

• *Breaking Through to Spiritual Maturity* (Regal Books). A curriculum for teaching the basic message of Freedom in Christ Ministries.

• *Discipleship Counseling* with videos (Regal Books). Discipleship and counseling are integrated practically with theology and psychology to help Christians resolve personal and spiritual conflicts through repentance.

• *Steps to Freedom in Christ* and interactive video (Regal Books). This discipleship counseling tool helps Christians resolve their personal and spiritual conflicts.

The Bondage Breaker® Series (Harvest House). Truth from the Word of God on specific issues—to bring you help and freedom in your life.

• *Praying by the Power of the Spirit*
• *Finding God's Will in Spiritually Deceptive Times*
• *Finding Freedom in a Sex-Obsessed World*
• *Unleashing God's Power in You*

Resources on Specific Issues

• *Getting Anger Under Control* with Rich Miller (Harvest House). Exposes the basis for anger and shows how you can control it.

• *Freedom from Fear* with Rich Miller (Harvest House). Discusses fear, anxiety, and anxiety disorders and reveals how you can be free from them.

• *Daily in Christ* (Harvest House). This popular daily devotional will encourage, motivate, and challenge you to experience the reality of *Christ in you.*

• *Breaking the Bondage of Legalism* with Rich Miller and Paul Travis (Harvest House). An exposure and explanation of legalism, the guilt and shame it brings, and how you can overcome it.

• *God's Power at Work in You* with Dr. Robert Saucy (Harvest House). A thorough analysis of sanctification, along with practical instruction on how you can grow in Christ.

- *A Way of Escape* (Harvest House). Exposes the bondage of sexual strongholds and shows you how they can be torn down in Christ.
- *The Seduction of Our Children* with Steve Russo (Harvest House). Reveals what teenagers are experiencing and how you as a parent can be equipped to help them.
- *Who I Am in Christ* (Regal Books). Thirty-six short chapters on who you are in Christ and how He meets your deepest needs.
- *Freedom from Addiction* with Mike Quarles (Regal Books).
- *One Day at a Time* with Mike Quarles (Regal Books).
- *The Christ-Centered Marriage* with Dr. Charles Mylander (Regal Books).
- *The Spiritual Protection of Our Children* with Peter and Sue Vander Hook (Regal Books).
- *Leading Teens to Freedom in Christ* with Rich Miller (Regal Books).
- *Finding Hope Again* with Hal Baumchen (Regal Books). Depression and how to overcome it.
- *Released from Bondage* with Judy King and Dr. Fernando Garzon (Thomas Nelson).
- *Freedom in Christ Bible* (Zondervan). A one-year discipleship study with notes in the Bible.
- *Blessed Are the Peacemakers* with Dr. Charles Mylander (Regal Books).
- *A Biblical Guide to Alternative Medicine* with Dr. Michael Jacobson (Regal Books).
- *Setting Your Church Free* with Dr. Charles Mylander (Regal Books).
- *Christ-Centered Therapy* with Dr. Terry and Julie Zuehlke (Zondervan).

The Victory Over the Darkness Series (Regal Books)
- *Overcoming a Negative Self-Image* with Dave Park
- *Overcoming Addictive Behavior* with Mike Quarles
- *Overcoming Doubt*
- *Overcoming Depression*

Contact information for Freedom in Christ Ministries:
9051 Executive Park Drive, Suite 503
Knoxville, TN 37923
Telephone: (865) 342-4000
E-mail: info@ficm.org
Web site: www.ficm.org

FREEDOM IN CHRIST
MINISTRIES

Conferences

- Spiritual Warfare and Biblical Worldview
- Discover the Treasure of Freedom in Christ
- Living Free in Christ
- Spiritual Protection for Your Children and Parenting
- Freedom in Christ Training Symposium
- Discipleship Counseling

Young Adult Event

- Worship Outside the Walls

Retreats

- Setting Your Church Free/Resolving Ministry Conflicts
- Christ-Centered Marriage/Resolving Marital Conflicts

Topical Study Tracks

- Freedom from Fear and Getting Anger Under Control
- Freedom from Addiction
- Freedom from Fear/Anxiety
- Ministering to the Sexually Abused

For more information on conferences, retreats,
and other events offered by Freedom in Christ Ministries,
please call our office at (865) 342-4005.

Freedom in Christ Ministries
9051 Executive Park Drive, Suite 503
Knoxville, TN 37923
www.ficm.org